Play
Bigger

Play Bigger

How Pirates, Dreamers, and Innovators Create
and Dominate Markets

Al Ramadan,

Dave Peterson,

Christopher Lochhead,

Kevin Maney

HARPER
BUSINESS

HarperCollins books may be purchased for educational, business, or sales promotional use. For information, please e-mail the Special Markets Department at SPsales@harpercollins.com.

FIRST EDITION

Designed by Fritz Metsch

Library of Congress Cataloging-in-Publication Data has been applied for.

ISBN: 978-0-06-240761-0

17 18 19 20   OV/RRD   10 9 8 7 6 5

Contents

Contents

Introduction:
From Bad Tuna to Play Bigger

Most books are by a soloist. The one you're holding is by a band.

Let me tell you our story.

First of all, Al Ramadan, Christopher Lochhead, and Dave Peterson are kind of nuts. I mean that in a sincerely affectionate way. Over the past dozen years, they've forged a relationship with each other unlike any I've seen between three men. Their business, Play Bigger,[1] gets paid large sums of money to help companies do exactly what's in this book. (So you're getting it cheap!) The whole company consists of just the three of them and their legendary ringleader Mary Forman ("admin" wouldn't do her justice), and they have no intention of hiring more employees, expanding globally, taking VC money, or trying to "disrupt" McKinsey. They don't have an office, preferring to work in bare feet and board shorts at Christopher's Santa Cruz, California, house with the hens out back, taking surfing breaks when the good waves roll in. They are refreshingly enthusiastic about everything and believe that there isn't a sentence that can't be made better by adding some version of "fuck" to it. When giving a presentation to, say, a board of directors, they can come across as an odd hybrid of business strategists, motivational speakers, and a family of pirates.

Most important, these guys are utterly bonded and connected to each other in life as well as in business, more like brothers than partners. On occasion, I have heard them half-jokingly call each other "honey."

All three grew up as outsiders—kids with rough edges who shouldn't have ever become so prosperous. Al was born in Australia, but his father was a blue-collar immigrant to that country from Cyprus. Christopher grew up in an English-speaking family originally from Scotland in French-speaking Montreal and thought he was stupid until he understood, in his twenties, that he was dyslexic. Dave was born in rural Iowa—a farm boy who stood out because he looked Asian. His Japanese mother had survived World War II firebombings and later married an American military man and crop-duster who brought her back home to that Iowa countryside. In the 1990s, Al, Christopher, and Dave wound up in Silicon Valley via separate, twisty routes. Before they succeeded, each of them at some point failed spectacularly—and their failures, to my mind, are a big reason why they know so much now. Or, as tech people might put it, the failures are a feature, not a bug.

I've known Al the longest. In the late 1990s, while I was writing for *USA Today* and covering the dot-com boom, I visited the company Al founded, Quokka Sports. It's still one of my favorite companies from that era. Al had previously been the chief technology officer for Australia's America's Cup racing team. From that experience, he realized that 1) emerging networked devices could capture all sorts of data about boats in a race and 2) yachting played terribly on television. Quokka was founded to take sports data and creatively display it on a website so fans of sailing or car racing or Olympic events could experience the sport in a whole new, immersive way. Quokka got everything right about how data was going to change the way fans consume sports—but it did so ten to twenty years too early. The data age of sports finally is taking hold in the mid-2010s. Quokka thrived in the dot-com era but wasn't strong enough to get through the dot-com crash of

2000, and in 2001 the company closed. By then Al had become a friend, and I continued to talk to him anytime I wrote about data and sports.

Al moved on to top positions at Macromedia, and then Adobe after Adobe bought Macromedia. While at Macromedia in 2001, Al first met Christopher and Dave.

In Silicon Valley circles, Christopher is a marketing legend. If Bruce Willis had been a chief marketing officer in the *Die Hard* movies—that would've been Christopher. He is brash, cocky, creative, and speaks so cleverly you'd think he was scripted by former *West Wing* writers. Since, as a teenager, he kept flunking out of school, Christopher never went to college and taught himself business by reading books like *Ogilvy on Advertising* and Geoffrey Moore's *Crossing the Chasm*. In the mid-1990s, he was an executive at a software company called Vantive, where Dave came to work with Christopher. Then, in the late 1990s, Christopher and I tangentially crossed paths when I wrote about Scient. That company was a rocket of the dot-com era, at one point hiring two thousand people within thirty-six months. It made its money consulting to companies about how to do business on the nascent Internet. Christopher was the company's chief marketing officer. Scient made the cover of *Forbes* magazine in 2000. Before the end of 2001, it was dead—a direct victim of the dot-com collapse. If you're a consulting company and your customers get nuked . . . you don't have anybody to consult to.

After Scient's demise, Christopher worked as a positioning consultant for a while, and partnered with Dave. One of their gigs in 2001 was to help Al figure out how to reposition Macromedia products—which, again, was when all three came together. Christopher had another significant run as a CMO, at Mercury Interactive. He and Dave repositioned the company and helped steer it to a 2006 acquisition by Hewlett-Packard for $4.5 billion. When Christopher joined Mercury, it was worth about $1 billion. As

Mercury's chief marketer, Christopher wanted the most talented person he knew by his side to run Mercury's communications. That was Dave.

I'd never had any connection to Dave. But now I would say that I think he can read people as well as anyone I've ever met. He would say he developed that capability as a defensive strategy when he was an Iowa kid who got picked on for his ethnicity. Instead of fighting back with fists or folding inward, Dave outsmarted his tormentors and took them down with words. He started out as a psychology major in college but switched to public relations because that's where all the girls were. At twenty-five, Dave moved to Silicon Valley to work for an ad agency, which had as one of its clients Vantive, where Christopher ran marketing. Before long, Christopher fired the agency and hired Dave to come to Vantive, and from that point on the two were pretty much glued together. Dave took a detour when he cofounded a company called GiveMeTalk!, thinking he'd make a fortune by creating a new market category he called "Internet talk radio." That turned out to be Dave's lesson in failure. To this day, almost no one has heard of GiveMeTalk! Dave and his cofounders were too early and later the space became this thing called podcasting. Dave then joined Christopher at Mercury, and that experience helped make Dave into a valuable entity in Silicon Valley. He had absorbed Christopher's marketing mojo and mixed it with his brand of people reading and aggressive execution (or, to use our technical term, Dave "gets shit done"), and companies wanted him. He ended up, for a while, running marketing for another software company, Coverity.

By 2006, both Al and Christopher had essentially retired. Dave was still at Coverity. Al and Christopher had second homes in Lake Tahoe, where they would get together on the ski slopes. Each did a little consulting and sat on a couple of boards, and were trying to figure out what to do next. Here's what Al told me: "One day Christopher and I were just riding the ski lift, and I said,

'Why the fuck are we doing this apart? This is nuts! You've got this skill, and I've got that skill. We really should think about doing this together.'" Al and Christopher combined forces, and not long after, Dave parted from Coverity and came aboard. The three quickly found that what they could do together was ten times better than what they might do individually. They're kind of like the Avengers, with different complementary superpowers: Christopher is the creative frontman; Al is the analytical business mind; Dave, as noted earlier, "gets shit done."

They needed a name for their advisory firm. Now, I wasn't around for this part, but knowing what I know now, I can imagine how the process went. It undoubtedly involved bourbon, IPAs, and a great deal of uncontrollable laughter. Somewhere along the line, the name Bad Tuna surfaced as a favorite. Eventually a more sober sensibility took over and they settled on Play Bigger, which captures the firm's ethos perfectly. However, Bad Tuna survives as their devilish alter ego. If you're ever working with these guys late at night, and a completely inappropriate idea surfaces, that's Bad Tuna talking.

One evening in 2013, I met Al and Dave for dinner at a San Francisco restaurant. That's where we first talked about a book, and before long I met with them again, this time including Christopher, to discuss the idea in more detail. I'd been writing about the technology industry since the mid-1980s, and their beliefs and philosophy about why certain start-ups wildly succeed struck me as fresh and interesting. From all their years at the top of companies, they had put together the concepts behind what we call category kings and category design, as well as tactics such as the POV and lightning strike. This was the Play Bigger intellectual property that they took to their clients. They wanted me to not just document what they already knew, but help shape the ideas further and deepen their understanding through journalistic and data research.

By that point, Play Bigger was gaining a reputation as advisors and coaches who could really make a difference in a company's fortunes. I was talking with Peggy Burke, a legendary brand designer for Silicon Valley companies (her firm designed Cisco's iconic bridge logo—and our book cover!), and she told me: "I can't overstate how much these guys are the heaviest lead foot on any gas pedal. They are the Mario Andrettis of marketing; of getting companies from zero to one hundred; of accelerating everything with their approach."

The clincher for me was why they wanted to do this work and produce this book. As I said earlier, they aren't looking to build a bigger business, so this book isn't a marketing tool. They believe they have something to contribute that can help entrepreneurs, investors, and executives, and even just regular people who are trying to build a great career. More times than I can count, Christopher pointed to *Ogilvy on Advertising* and *Crossing the Chasm*, and said that if David Ogilvy and Geoff Moore had not written those books, he wouldn't be where he is today. He and the other guys truly hope this will be such a book for the next generation.

So I bought in, and we all spent hundreds of hours debating these ideas, mostly in Santa Cruz with the hens out back. (Unfortunately, I'm not really a surfer. Yet.) We gathered and crunched data to find characteristics of category kings, and then researched dozens of case studies and interviewed founders, CEOs, and venture capitalists to find out how category kings and category design really work.

From all indications, I easily plugged into the Play Bigger milieu. I grew up in Binghamton, New York, in circumstances the guys could relate to, shaped by difficult years after my father died when I was nine. I've spent my adult life telling stories about the technology industry in books, for newspapers and magazines, and on television—all from either Washington, D.C., or New York City, preferring to observe Silicon Valley without being *of* Silicon

Valley. And as a child of upstate New York, I have never stopped playing hockey. Al, Christopher, and Dave can kick my ass on the waves, but put us on some frozen water and they will be begging for mercy.

All in all, that's why this book is by a band. Play Bigger already had a metaphorical lead singer (Christopher), bass player (Al), and drummer (Dave). I brought along my guitar, and it all clicked. The songs on this album wouldn't exist without all of us. The book is a true collaboration.

Now I am going to shut up. The voice you hear through the rest of the book will be our collective harmony. At times in the book, we will turn to a specific experience from Al, Christopher, or Dave, and we'll talk about it in the third person: Al did this at Macromedia or Christopher and Dave have a story from Mercury . . . and so on. All in all, consider everything to be coming from all of us.

Kevin Maney
New York, NY
2015

Part I

The Category King Economy

Creation Wins

Legendary Questions

What do Facebook, Google, Salesforce.com, Uber, VMware, Netflix, IKEA, Birds Eye, 5-hour Energy, and Pixar have in common?

In what way does Apple work like 165-year-old glass company Corning?

What all-too-common mistake did Microsoft make—and repeat over and over—when it wasted billions of dollars on Zune, Windows Mobile, Bing, and Microsoft Stores?

How do you explain why some start-ups last and build value while others shoot up and then flame out?

Why was Elvis not just the King, but a category king?

And what can all of this teach us about enduring success in the twenty-first-century economy—in both good times and downturns?

The key to each has to do with creating, developing, and dominating new categories of products and services.

Stick around and we'll tell you how that's done.

True Stories of Kings and Kingdoms

Category kings are all around us. They create entirely new categories of business, or entirely new ways of doing things. For this book, we studied category kings, analyzed data about them, and interviewed founders of many. These are the companies that shape our lives and alter the future. As we like to say, they play bigger than other companies.

Category kings are not a recent phenomenon. Before the 1920s, there existed no such category as "frozen foods." Clarence Birdseye—yep, that was actually his name—created it. Like many category creators through the ages, Birdseye was an outsider. Born in Brooklyn, New York, in 1886, he spent a lot of time on his family's farm on Long Island and developed a passion for taxidermy (not a hobby many kids have these days). That led him to a job as a naturalist for the U.S. government, which eventually took him to Labrador, in Canada's northeastern corner. Birdseye watched the Inuit people catch fish and toss them on the ice, where the fish flash-froze, retaining their flavor and texture. When Birdseye returned to the United States, he experimented by flash-freezing fish between cakes of dry ice, and then realized the process also worked for vegetables. He started a company—at first called General Seafoods—to make and sell this new category of product.

As he built his company, Birdseye realized he had to design and build the category itself, because before Birdseye, there was no ecosystem that would get frozen food from a factory to consumers, and no demand for frozen food because consumers didn't even know they might want it. He developed freezer cars for railroads and sold rail operators on the idea. He developed freezer cases for grocers and convinced them that frozen food would increase sales. He even convinced DuPont to invent cellophane. And he ran ads that positioned frozen vegetables as something different from canned vegetables. One early *Life* magazine ad—by then under the Birds Eye brand—showed a woman in pearls lounging on a pillow eating Birds Eye spinach, implying that only commoners put up with canned spinach. Frozen food was not just *better* than canned food—it was *different* from canned food. Birdseye's work took a couple of decades to pay off, but it takes time to build and dominate categories—and it took a lot more time then than it does now. Of course, almost a century later, Birds Eye is still a huge brand in frozen foods.[1]

Clarence Birdseye has more in common than you might think with the founders of Uber.

Uber is a category king of recent vintage. Not very long ago, we all lived with an age-old problem: in most cities, taxi service sucked. If you walked out to a given street corner, you had no idea if a taxi might happen by in a few minutes or, well, never. Yet there didn't seem to be an alternative way to get an instant car ride, so people didn't seek one out. We had an old, ongoing problem, but we didn't really know it was a problem that could be solved in a new way.

On a snowy night in Paris in 2008, Travis Kalanick and Garrett Camp, in the city for a European tech conference, stood roadside getting wetter and colder as they tried in vain to hail a cab. Kalanick and Camp were, separately, already reasonably successful tech entrepreneurs. Kalanick had started an online content-delivery company, Red Swoosh, which got bought by Akamai Technologies for $20 million. Camp had done better, founding StumbleUpon—a content discovery site—and selling it to eBay for $75 million.[2] They were looking for a next idea for a company—perhaps something they'd do together—and while freezing and frustrated in Paris, they talked of solving this taxi problem. Apple's iPhone had been introduced less than a year earlier, changing the way we think about mobile technology and services. Why, Kalanick and Camp wondered, couldn't you pull out your smartphone, push a button, and get picked up by a car?

Back home in San Francisco, the pair experienced the problem anew. Hailing a cab in that town was like trying to get a bartender's attention in a jam-packed nightclub. So Kalanick and Camp went to work on their idea, and launched their service in the summer of 2010 in San Francisco. As millions of users now know, a customer's iPhone app would, at the push of a button, send a dispatch to drivers, showing the customer's location. Drivers—not taxis, but moonlighters driving their own cars—would have their own version of the app on a phone, allowing them to see dispatches and respond. The system would store customers' credit card information, so paying for the ride could be easy and safe for everyone involved. Kalanick and Camp originally called this service Uber-Cab, and later dropped the second part.

Half a year later, investors were lining up to give Uber money. Benchmark Capital put in $10 million. Some famous names such as Jay-Z and Jeff Bezos invested. Uber expanded to other cities. As it grew, Uber at the same time did something extremely important: Uber made all of us aware that we had a taxi problem—and that the problem had a new solution. Uber did this through the way it designed the company and its service. It did this through its messaging to the public. And it did this through confrontation. Every time the taxi industry tried to stop Uber, the scuffle made people more aware of Uber. In London, taxi drivers protested Uber by going on strike. When riders couldn't get cabs, they signed up for Uber at a rate eight times higher than before the strike. As Uber was developing its service and its company, it was defining this new category of problem and inserting it into our brains.

Within a couple of years, Kalanick, by then Uber's CEO and public face, understood that he could frame an even larger problem that Uber could solve. All of personal transportation was too expensive and too messy, particularly in cities. Plus, too many cars lead to traffic jams and pollution. Those were big problems that never had a good solution. But what if, Kalanick asked all of us, fewer cars could serve more people? What if his service could get so big, reliable, and cheap that in many places using Uber could become more desirable than owning a car? He wanted to make "transportation that's as reliable as running water," he told interviewers. And, by the way, that transportation wouldn't only move people around town—it could move anything. It could deliver stuff. Uber was designing its service and its company and, at the same time, a bigger category the company could define and ultimately dominate.[3]

By 2014, Uber was getting what seemed like preposterous valuations from investors. In June 2014 it was valued at $17 billion. By December the number hit $40 billion. Six months later it topped $50 billion. If you looked at Uber's business at the time, you would've concluded that its investors were out of their minds. But if you looked at the enormity of the problem Uber had teed itself up to solve, $40 billion or $50 billion seemed cheap in the long run. Uber was creating a category of business that never before existed, and the company put it into our minds that it uniquely understood the problem and could craft a solution. Where a half-dozen years before there had been nothing, Uber was creating a whopper of a category, and making itself king. That's what investors were paying for: the potential of this new category and the belief that Uber would reign as its king for a long time. In 2015, Uber was still private—a sign that despite all its notoriety, Uber at five years old was still developing its category. Our data research shows that smart companies typically go public about the time their category takes wing—usually six to ten years after the company's founding.

In the twenty-first century, new category kings are being founded all the time, and at a faster rate than ever. A company called Sensity Systems is but one example. It started on a category creation path after serial entrepreneur Hugh Martin took over what was then a tiny company making LED lights. Martin was an outsider to the lighting industry. He'd previously run a biotech company, a telecommunications company, and a video game company—but never a lighting company. He saw an interesting opportunity in LED lights. LEDs run on the same voltage—five volts, DC—as computers, networking equipment, and digital sensors. That means that LEDs can essentially digitize light fixtures,

changing the lighting industry just as much as music and pho-
tography were changed by becoming digital. In fact, lights can be
embedded with sensors that pull in information about air quality,
motion, sound, or weather. And since the lights can communicate
over wireless networks, the LEDs can be networked together to
share information or collect massive amounts of data. Lighting
networks would then be able to track the number of cars in a mall
parking lot, or, for police, light networks could detect gunshots
with far better accuracy than current technology. Down the road,
Martin could envision a globally connected light platform.

We had the pleasure of working with Martin on defining and
planning out the category he envisioned—a process we call category design. Martin and this team settled on a name for the category: Light Sensory Network, or LSN. Martin started evangelizing
the category at the same time as he was building his company.
He wanted potential customers to first understand the problems a
Light Sensory Network could solve. And if they wanted the problem solved, who were they going to call? Of course: the company
that defined and made itself synonymous with category—Sensity.
Without this kind of thinking, Sensity would've been just another undifferentiated smart lighting company. But it became the
leading Light Sensory Network company.[4] Huge global companies
entered the business of LED lights and sensors—General Electric,
Philips, Samsung, LG. But Sensity, which by 2015 had signed up
GE and Cisco as partners, wasn't trying to beat them by making *better* sensor-loaded LEDs. It planned to win by marketing
something *different*, focused on the network and data. If Sensity
executes well, it will reign as an enduring category king of Light
Sensory Networks.

Again, this will take time—probably a decade. There's no
guarantee the strategy will work. A lot of factors will come into
play, many that Martin or Sensity can't control. But still, the
chances of Sensity winning are much greater because it is doing

the groundwork to design and develop its category. Sensity improved the odds that it will play bigger.

Category Kings Defined

The most exciting companies create. They give us new ways of living, thinking, or doing business, many times solving a problem we didn't know we had—or a problem we didn't pay attention to because we never thought there was another way. Before Uber, we hailed a cab by standing perilously close to traffic with an arm in the air. After Uber, that just seemed dumb.

These companies don't only invent something to sell us. They are not making products or services that just incrementally improve on whatever came before. They don't sell us *better*. The most exciting companies sell us *different*. They introduce the world to a new *category* of product or service—like Clarence Birdseye's frozen food, or Uber's on-demand transportation. They replace our current point of view on the world with a new point of view. They make what came before seem outdated, clunky, inefficient, costly, or painful.

We hear a lot about "disruption." It's a holy word in the tech industry, like maybe you should genuflect when someone says it. But disruption is a by-product, not a goal. Legendary companies create new categories that generate a gravitational pull on the market. Customers rush to a new category because it makes sense to them. In some cases, people leave an old category behind, and their departure sucks the life out of it. In that way, sure, new categories disrupt old categories. But for the smartest pirates, dreamers, and innovators on the planet, disruption is never the goal. Creation is the goal. Elvis Presley didn't set out to "disrupt" jazz. He set out to create rock and roll—a product that came from his soul. Rock was different, not better, than jazz. But over time, as young audiences embraced rock, they left big-band jazz and crooners behind. The by-product of Elvis's creation was disruption.

Sometimes, booming new categories don't disrupt anything at all. Airbnb created a new category of on-demand places to stay, but as of this writing no one—including and especially cofounder and CEO Brian Chesky—is predicting the new category will lead to the collapse of the hotel industry.

Our term for the companies that create, develop, and dominate new categories is *category kings*. Importantly, category kings are not necessarily the companies that first hatch an idea or patent an invention. A single cool product launched into the universe doesn't make a category king. Category kings take it upon themselves to design a great product, a great company, and a great category at the same time. A category king willfully defines and develops its category, setting itself up as the company that dominates that category for a long time.

From time to time, the technology industry gets caught up in hype about soaring valuations of start-ups. But like disruption, valuations are an outcome, not a strategy. A billion-dollar valuation of a company that is not a category king is likely to be fleeting. A billion-dollar valuation of a category king that is creating, developing, and dominating a new category is often a bargain, in good economies or bad.

Category kings are the explosive and enduring companies that create great value over time—Amazon.com, Salesforce.com, Facebook, Google. They do this by opening up a category with vast potential—we use the term *category potential*—and set themselves up to take most of the economics of the whole category. Category kings, the data show, usually eat up 70 percent to 80 percent of the category's profits and market value. Our data science analysis of U.S. venture capital–backed tech start-ups founded from 2000 to 2015 shows that category kings earned 76 percent of the market capitalization of their entire market categories. Category kings become some of the most famous brands because they become the symbol of the whole category—Xerox, Google, IKEA. The category king literally owns the problem it is solving. And for that reason, a category king is almost impossible to dislodge from its position in the category. Customers are too wedded to it. That's why Microsoft spent $10 billion on Bing yet never made a dent in Google's share of search. It's almost always futile to try to unseat a category king that's not screwing up.[5]

This book is about the strategy that builds category kings. Following this strategy doesn't make it certain you'll become a category king, but it will improve your odds. And we believe it will at least help you play bigger than you otherwise might. As we'll show, a category king strategy is important and effective when the economy is roaring, and perhaps even more powerful when downturns cripple runner-up competitors. Some of the great category kings have been built during some of the "worst" times—Google in the early 2000s right after the dot-com crash; Airbnb in 2008 as financial markets melted; Birds Eye amid the Great Depression.[6]

Category kings are often the companies that get the most attention in the media and from investors and the public. Facebook defined and developed a new kind of social network that was based on your real life. We'll discuss later how that was different, not better, compared to social networks before it. Netflix started by creating the category of DVDs by mail (*different* from Blockbuster) and later created the category of streaming movies. Pixar designed the category of computer-generated movies. Airbnb, Tesla, Snapchat, and Twitter are recent category kings in consumer-facing markets. The enterprise technology space is full of category kings, too. Salesforce.com developed the cloud-based sales automation category. VMware defined and dominated a category of computer virtualization. Workday, Zenefits, NetSuite, and Slack are among the new category kings of business services.

Most category kings are once-in-a-founder's-lifetime achievements. A rare few individuals have proven to be master category king creators. One of the best of all time, as you might imagine, was Steve Jobs, especially during his second go-round at Apple. He led the creation of three important new categories: digital music (with the iPod and iTunes), smartphones (iPhone), and tablets (iPad). Elon Musk made Tesla Motors into the category king of electric cars and SpaceX into the category king of private spaceflight, incredibly doing that for both companies at the same time. Jeff Bezos started out making Amazon.com the category king of online retail, and repeated that success with e-book readers (Kindle) and cloud-based computing services (Amazon Web Services). A lesser-known but no less prolific creator of category kings is Seattle entrepreneur Rich Barton. He had a hand in founding Expedia, Zillow, and Glassdoor.

As noted with Birds Eye, category kings aren't just a connected-age technology phenomenon. When Chrysler introduced the mini-van in 1983, it created—and then dominated for three decades—a new category of personal vehicle. Bob Pittman's MTV and Ted Turner's CNN were once category kings. Boeing created the category of jet airliner with its 707 in 1958. Sometimes category kings aren't even a business, yet they define and develop something new in our way of life. Peter Drucker was the category king of management thinking. And of course as we've mentioned, there was Elvis Presley, the category king of rock and roll. Those individuals were not just better than what came before; they were very different from what came before.

Finally, category kings don't only come from Silicon Valley, or the United States. Global category kings have been born in all corners of the planet. IKEA created a new category of cheap, stylish, do-it-yourself furniture out of the tiny town of Älmhult in Sweden, and there's nothing else like it. Estonia gave birth to Skype, which developed the category of Internet phone calls. Australia has given us Atlassian, the category king of collaborative technology for teams that build software. In some businesses, cultural differences or national borders provide an opportunity to create a geography-defined category king. Alibaba built a gigantic category-dominating company by defining itself, essentially, as the Amazon.com of China. Flipkart did the same in India. Neither defined and developed the online retailing category, but they defined and developed online retailing in a different way to address and dominate a vast home market.

For this book, we researched the category kings we just mentioned, and many more, and we'll discuss them in detail in later chapters.

Category King Economics

The economic advantages gained by a category king are staggering, and the trajectory is steeper and faster than ever. The reason has little to do with investor speculation that might prove fickle. It has everything to do with powerful technology trends that are only gaining momentum. The trends are changing the way the most astute venture capitalists invest, which in turn has shaped how entrepreneurs think about the companies they start. Category king economics are influencing CEOs as they consider new offerings and future directions, and affecting the way marketers position and engineers build products. Anybody planning a career needs to be aware of category king economics.

In his 2014 book, *Zero to One*, super-investor Peter Thiel unequivocally celebrated monopolies, and made it clear that those are the companies he wants to invest in. "Every monopoly is unique, but they usually share some combination of the following characteristics: proprietary technology, network effects, economies of scale, and branding." As you'll see, he's describing category kings—the companies that take all the economics out of a category. Thiel goes on to say, "All happy companies are different: each one earns a monopoly by solving a unique problem. All failed companies are the same: they failed to escape competition." By Thiel's definition, category kings are the happy companies.[7]

For years, Mike Maples, one of Silicon Valley's legendary investors, has talked about seeking to put his money into "thunder lizards." That's his term for category kings. "A thunder lizard is a game-changing company that will massively outperform the rest of the industry," he tells the class that he teaches at Stanford University. "Thunder lizards are rare. If in a given year there are 10,000 startups that get funded by angels and 1,500 get a Series A funding, then 80 companies will likely do well—but only 12 will be a thunder lizard."[8]

In Silicon Valley, we've watched venture capitalists (VCs) increasingly adopt a category king investment philosophy. Paul Martino of Bullpen Capital notes that VCs used to have a "me-too" strategy: if a start-up hit it big and opened up a hot new category, the many VC firms in Silicon Valley assumed that there was room for a lot of winners in that category. So every firm would invest in some company—any company!—in the emerging category. But in this century, that phrase—"room for a lot of winners in that market"—needs to be banished to the Home for the Criminally Insane. As Martino tells us, it's now apparent that one company wins big and dominates a healthy category, and the rest struggle, get acquired or perish. That means that as soon as one company appears to be the category king, the smart money competes to invest in that company, bidding up its value. That realization among investors is a reason valuations of new category kings spiked so drastically in the 2010s. On the flip side, while me-too companies can get funding early on, they quickly find they have trouble getting new rounds from high-quality investors who understand category king economics. A lot of the me-toos are a lost cause waiting to happen.[9] Bryan Roberts at Venrock, another top-tier VC, tries to spot potential category kings early. "A category king tends to have broken open a new space, and that often means a big risk element early on—something most people think you can't surmount, or that if you do surmount, no one will care," he told us. A company like Snapchat might fall into that latter category. Early on, a lot of people wondered why anyone except teenagers would care about a service that disappears their selfies. But once a category king proves its category works, as Snapchat did, "things go from non-consensus to consensus very quickly, but by then you [the company] have some competitive advantage that's hard to surmount." In Roberts's view, category kings win big— and these days, they win fast.[10] Meanwhile, Jim Goetz of Sequoia Capital directly advertises his category creation philosophy: "We seek mission-driven founders who can build a great company and category at the same time."

Various studies point to the power of category kings. Eddie Yoon, a principal at the Cambridge Group, in 2011 published a piece in *Harvard Business Review* titled "Category Creation Is the Ultimate Growth Strategy." His firm had run an analysis of the top twenty companies on *Fortune*'s 2010 list of fastest-growing companies. Those twenty companies received an average of $3.40 in incremental market capitalization for every dollar of revenue growth. But half of those top twenty were category creators, Yoon determined, and those ten companies got $5.60 in incremental market cap for every dollar of revenue growth. "Wall Street exponentially rewards the category creation companies," Yoon wrote.[11] In 2014, consulting giant McKinsey published an article titled "Grow Fast or Die Slow." McKinsey analyzed three thousand software and online companies from 1980 to 2012. It identified a small slice of remarkable companies as "Supergrowers," which pretty much overlaps with our definition of category kings, and proclaimed that wildly fast out-of-the-starting-gate growth predicts long-term success. Category kings, once established, are almost impossible to displace.

Why is this happening with so much velocity now, especially since category kings have always been a part of the business landscape?

The ubiquity of networks, cheap cloud-based distribution, and lightning-fast word of mouth through social media is intensifying a winner-take-all economy—especially when we're talking about digital products and services. Keep in mind that in 1999, about 400 million people were connected to the Internet. By 2015 that number had rocketed to 3 billion, on its way to 4 billion by 2020. And by 2020 the planet is expected to have 6 billion smartphones in use. At the same time, tens of billions of things like cars, lights, industrial sensors, thermostats, and dog collars are getting connected to networks, while industries that were never digital (taxis, hotels, medicine) are quickly becoming digital. This Internet of Things will make almost everything part of the global network. Since networks give everyone from anyplace access to the perceived best in any category, the vast majority choose the leader and leave the second- or third-best behind. It's the dark side of the "long tail" concept pundits have been talking about for more than a decade: In any category of product or service, one entity gets to be the big and valuable dog, while all the rest wind up in the economically challenging tail. The category king dogs unequivocally wag the second-tier tails.

Once a company wins a position as category king, a flywheel of benefits opens a gap between the leader and the rest. The leader, for example, increasingly has the best data. In today's world, data is power. All those transactions on Amazon give the company valuable insights about its customers, inventory, prices—everything. Same with every ride through Uber, every movie chosen on Netflix, every entry on Salesforce.com. As the leader amasses data, the data becomes an unfair advantage—a gap that the followers can't hope to close. Also, the best employees want to work for the category king. The best partners want to sign deals with the category king. Outside developers want to develop for the category king. The best investors want to put in their money and the best investment bankers want to work on the IPO. As a category king pulls far ahead economically, it has the wherewithal to make acquisitions that vault it even further into the lead. The economic power of a category king just builds and builds.

In late 2014, one tech industry analyst, Michael Walkley of Canaccord Genuity, looked at the state of profits of smartphone companies and found that Apple took in 93 percent of the industry's total profits.[12] Imagine that! Of all the world's smartphone makers, one company—the category king—claimed almost all of the economics. Like it or not, there is increasingly no middle class in business. The wealth goes to the kings. A second-place prince—such as Lyft or Samsung—can get a tidy share of the economics. The rest of the players get relegated to the life of serfs in the category king's empire.

In the mid-2010s, the media became obsessed with fast-rising valuations of tech start-ups. Some of the numbers might've been driven by financial market conditions, which of course can change with the wind. But the big picture, the exuberance has been driven by foundational changes in technology and the economy, and exacerbated by category king economics. If you look closely, you'll see that the highest-valuation start-ups are almost always established or emerging category kings.

Through data, we captured a moment in time that shows the velocity of growth and the yawning gap between kings and the rest. We analyzed valuation data on thousands of tech start-ups, and found that winning companies born between 2009 and 2014 got to superhigh valuations three times faster than companies started in the early 2000s. In other words, in just over a decade, the growth rate of the value of high-growth tech start-ups nearly tripled. But unlike in the tech boom of the late 1990s, that rising tide was floating the yachts while sinking the dinghies.[13] A category's non-kings struggled. Our data science research found that a six-year-old start-up that wasn't yet a king had almost zero chance of becoming one.

Here's the category king gap in a nutshell: Uber was valued at
$51 billion in late 2015, while at about the same time the number
two in that space, Lyft, was valued about 25 times lower, at $2 bil-
lion. The rest of that category was barely noticeable. Perhaps the
actual values were unsustainably high; perhaps not. But our attention is on the relative value—on Uber being worth 25 times more
than Lyft. Investors looked at the future value of the category of
on-demand personal transportation and saw one company—the
king, Uber—taking most of it.

We started writing this book amid a frothy up cycle in the tech
industry. We have no idea whether by the time you're reading this
the tech boom will have tipped into a down cycle. But we're certain that the dynamics and strategies in this book are perpetual.
In flush times, a company needs to think like a category king to
outrun and outmaneuver all the other competitors that will get
funded. In rough times, when money is tight, a king might be
the only survivor in a given category. In general, a down cycle is a
fantastic opportunity for a category king to dispense with all of its
underfunded challengers and come out of the cycle more powerful
than ever.

In short, any time—up or down or middling—is a good time
to get smarter instead of hoping to get luckier. And thinking like
a category king is a smart way to improve your odds of success,
instead of leaving it to chance. This is what we mean by playing
bigger.

Introducing Category Design

If you play poker, you know of Greg Raymer. He bounced around
the Midwest while growing up, got a master's degree in biochem-
istry from the University of Minnesota, graduated from the University of Minnesota Law School in 1992, then worked as a patent
attorney for Pfizer. He'd played lots of poker in college—"we were

all pretty pathetic," he recalls. And then, while working in Chicago, he decided it was time to learn to play well. He read poker books and started entering tournaments, perfecting his game as he played. In 2004, he won the World Series of Poker—a $5 million prize. At the World Series of Poker the following year, he did something unprecedented in a game that seems to involve so much luck: he followed up his first-place victory by finishing in the top tier again, taking home more than $300,000. By 2013 he'd made more than $7.4 million playing poker. Uh, and he quit his day job.

We talked to Raymer about how someone can increase his or her odds in a game that has so many factors that can't be controlled. (Seriously, we don't want to talk to technology people all the time.) "A lot of people don't think about luck and skill properly," he told us. Most people, he explained, think of luck and skill in any particular endeavor as a zero-sum continuum—a straight line that puts luck at one end and skill at the other. That would mean that if you'd say that an outcome is determined by 40 percent luck, it must be 60 percent skill; or if it's 90 percent luck, then the outcome must rely on only 10 percent skill. But luck and skill, Raymer insisted, "are not on the same axis." And that makes all the difference.[14]

Of course, Raymer used poker to illustrate. There is a great amount of luck involved in which cards you get. But there's also a great amount of skill in deciding what to do with those cards, the bets you place, the way you conduct yourself at the table. On the luck side, the odds for everyone around the table are the same. On any given hand, you might be terribly unlucky, and there would be nothing much you could do to win. But the most skillful players essentially better their odds over time. If the odds are the same for everyone, more skill results in better decisions with the cards you're dealt, and ultimately gives you a better chance of winning. "You have to be realistic about how much luck is involved in whatever you're doing and after that kind of ignore it," Raymer said. "Then you have to say, what's the smartest decision I can make and ignore results in the short run because they are irrelevant." Raymer's consistent success shows that good outcomes don't happen by accident even in chaotic multidimensional games like poker.

Or business.

In business, the odds are stacked against any one company becoming a category king. A company can do everything right yet fall victim to outside forces it can't control. We learned this in the late 1990s before forming Play Bigger, sometimes painfully. Al carved out a brilliant new category of digital immersive sports at Quokka, but technology and broadband networks didn't catch up to his vision fast enough, and the company didn't survive. Christopher had a similar experience at Scient, helping to build a leader in e-commerce consulting that then fell victim to the impact of the dot-com crash on its clients.

If it's become highly desirable for a company to become a category king—if we're in an era when the category king wins big and everyone else goes home—why wouldn't you do everything you can to boost your odds? If the odds are the same for every company, your company needs to make decisions and implement a strategy that gives it the best chance to beat the odds and beat competing companies. An occasional category king might be almost entirely the result of luck. But most category kings are not an accident. Many start out with a lucky break, addressing a seemingly small problem that later taps into big demand at exactly the right time. But those companies usually develop and dominate their new categories by making skillful decisions and executing on a purposeful plan.

We see the emergence of a new discipline in business. We call the discipline *category design*. It is emerging today in much the way engineers embraced product design in the 1980s to make sure individual products had the best chance of succeeding—of beating the odds. In the early 2000s, companies adopted experience design—a discipline a step up from product design, developed as a way to make sure the mix of hardware, software, and usability together gave the user the best experience possible. Experience design is yet another way to improve the odds of winning in a nutty marketplace.

Category design involves creating a great product (along with its experience), a great company, and a great category at the same time. It is a broad, deep discipline that impacts every part of a company and its leadership team.

We've practiced category design as executives at our own companies in the past, including Macromedia and Mercury Interactive. With help from our category thinking, Macromedia was sold for $3.5 billion and Mercury for $4.5 billion. We've also researched and analyzed the category king activity around us, particularly in Silicon Valley. More recently, as advisors and coaches, we've worked on category design with a diverse group of companies —in each case with the goal of increasing the chances that the company will have a significant and enduring impact. Our goal in this book is to give you tools to better your odds of getting to your own great outcome.

Bad Category Design: A Cautionary Tale

We can also tell you what category design is not. For instance, it's not what Jawbone practiced. Impressively, three times in its first sixteen years of its existence, Jawbone came up with cool innovations that created a brand-new product category. Not many start-ups ever do that. But three times, Jawbone failed to develop and dominate the category it created. Not many start-ups do that, either.

Jawbone's story began like so many others in Silicon Valley: at Stanford University. A student, Alexander Asseily, working on his senior thesis, drew up plans for a wrist-worn cell phone that wire-lessly connected to a headset. That turned into a business plan for a company initially called AliphCom—later changed to Jawbone. While working on the wrist-worn product, which never got made, AliphCom developed headset technology that could be used to suppress background noise while clearly picking up the user's voice. That led to U.S. Defense Department contracts, a few prod-uct development missteps, and then, in 2007, a breakthrough de-vice: a small headset that could wirelessly connect to a cell phone using Bluetooth and suppress surrounding noise. Called Jawbone, the product came along just as states were passing laws saying phone calls in cars had to be hands-free. The whole situation was just what category creation is all about. The Jawbone was an agenda-setting solution for a clear problem at the right time. The investment community knew it. As sales of Jawbone devices took flight, top-tier venture capitalists lined up to give the company money. An IPO seemed likely. But the company didn't cement the Jawbone device's position. It didn't systematically develop the cate-gory of high-quality hands-free calling, didn't develop the public's demand for this solution, and didn't get overwhelming publicity and credit for creating the leading solution to the problem. As competitors came out with competing products, Jawbone seemed to the public like just another wireless headset. Put another way, if someone in 2009 decided she needed a wireless headset, the auto-matic thought probably wasn't that she needed a *Jawbone* headset. More likely, she'd have thought: I'll go to Best Buy and compare products and prices of wireless headsets and then decide which one to purchase. If consumers are doing that, the category has no king. In retrospect, Jawbone had the opportunity to develop a great product, great company, and great category at the same time, but didn't. It fell short on category design. Jawbone sales veered south by 2009, and a planned IPO was put on hold.

So that was the company's first category whiff. But then in

2010, Jawbone (by then the name of the company itself) came out with a category-defining Bluetooth speaker, the Jambox. *Fortune* magazine even wrote that Jambox was "creating an entirely new consumer category." And yet Jawbone again left category design on the table. Other companies, such as Bose and Logitech, soon matched the features and quality of the Jambox and the market flooded with competing products. By 2015, the Jambox had only 5 percent of its category's market share.[15]

Finally, Jawbone seemed poised to invent the wearable fitness tracker category with a device called the UP3. This time, the product didn't get out in the planned time frame, and a start-up company—Fitbit—barged in and stole the category. In 2015, Fitbit had become the king of wearable fitness trackers, and sopped up 68 percent of the category's market share in North America. The Fitbit brand became synonymous with the category in a way that the Jawbone headset, Jambox speaker, and UP3 tracker never did. The Jawbone company, inventive as it was, could have become an Amazon or Apple. But its performance failed to live up to its promise, and we believe that while the company got product innovation right, it fell down on category design.

We can tell you some other things category design is not.

It's not any of this first-mover advantage bullshit that has been a Silicon Valley calling card since the 1990s. Being first to invent something can be fantastically important, but it doesn't mean squat if you don't define and develop the category. Jawbone is one proof point, but we could cite hundreds. Apple didn't invent any of the product categories it came to dominate. Facebook wasn't the first social network. Tesla didn't make the first electric car. But they all made something different from what came before, and built a category that pulled in customers and made them desire the product. The first inventor is an innovator to be thanked. The first to define and develop a category is a category king to be followed.

Category design is not just engineering. Too many people in Silicon Valley believe that building a great product is enough, and that the market will find it and flock to it. That's a disease that has infected even the best and brightest minds. In fact, the best product doesn't always win the category. Different wins. Great category thinking wins. Best product gets you an award at a TechCrunch conference.

Category design is also not just marketing. Category design is a company-wide strategy. It involves the CEO and top management, product designers, engineers, sales, marketing, PR, partners—and often customers and users, too. We've heard CEOs sing the refrain: "We make shit and sell shit and everything else is bullshit." Well, good luck with that. While you're making shit and selling shit, someone else will define your category and steal it from you.

Category design isn't just positioning or branding. We have great respect for the seminal 1970s book *Positioning*, by Al Ries and Jack Trout.[16] Their sense of positioning as a necessary discipline was on the mark for the late twentieth century. But in this century of mobile/social/cloud, dynamics have changed, and positioning is only one part of category design. And as for branding—we call branding agencies "tattoo parlors." You don't want to wake up with Mike Tyson's tattoo on your face, so don't let someone else tattoo you. Brands don't make a category king. Category design does.

Here's How We Did This Book

The three of us in Play Bigger came into this book project with our intimate experiences and gut feelings about category-based strategy. We had been at the top levels of companies, some of which became category kings for a period of time. We came together to advise companies about the ideas behind category design, and as we did, we learned more.

To test our ideas, we started by crunching data so we could understand both the game and the timing of the game. We pulled in data on thousands of public and private technology companies started between 2000 and 2015, and sorted for valuation and market-domination trends. This helped us identify companies that defined, developed, and then dominated a category of product or service that did not exist previously. In our reckoning, there were thirty-five giant category kings created from 2000 to 2015. Others have emerged since then.

Once we had those thirty-five, we researched them to look for patterns. In this way, we could check our beliefs against the characteristics and best practices of living, breathing category kings. As it started to become clear to us what made a king, we looked for other kings that wouldn't have shown up in our study—older companies like Birds Eye, or emerging kings like Sensity—and added those to our bag of research. We also looked at companies that tried but failed to become category kings, or somehow lost their category crown.

As common characteristics emerged, we sorted them into buckets and drew out principles. The buckets make up the chapters of the rest of this book.

Ten Reasons You Shouldn't Read the Rest of This Book

1. You think the company with the best product wins.
2. You believe there is room for a lot of winners in a market, that a rising tide lifts all boats, and other feel-good hippy garbage.
3. You're okay with being good enough.
4. You're afraid to lean forward on your skis while you're already going 80 miles per hour downhill.
5. You're an engineer who thinks marketing is what you do when you have a bush-league product.

6. You're a classically trained marketer who thinks reach and frequency win the game.
7. You believe heady competition is the ideal.
8. You think an IPO is just a financial event.
9. You think you're not in the technology business and never will be, so you don't think tech industry dynamics apply— you know, the way the taxi industry used to think.
10. You work at SAP.[17]

2

Category Is the New Strategy

Why Categories

A brief history of books that marked milestones in market thinking:

Thirty-five years ago, at the height of the TV age, two marketing experts published *Positioning*—about maneuvering a product to the top of an existing market.[1]

In 1991, as the microprocessor brought computing to the masses, another book, *Crossing the Chasm*, focused on the marketing challenges of innovation—developing a new product for an existing market.[2]

In 1997, with the dot-com explosion taking hold, *The Innovator's Dilemma* introduced the concept of disruptive innovation—how a radically innovative product upends an existing market.[3]

Today the powerful transforming force is the category—creating a new market for a new product, often (but not always) from a new company. A great message, a great product, a great innovation—these things are no longer enough on their own. Now it's critical to develop a great new market category in concert with building a great company and product.

We see a link between brain science and the business strategy of modern category kings. Let us explain . . .

The dynamics described in *Positioning*, *Chasm*, and *Innovator's Dilemma* haven't gone away. If anything, they've been kicked into hyperspeed. *Positioning* almost quaintly describes a 1970s landscape where "there are just too many products, too many companies, and too much marketing noise." And that was when most TVs pulled in three channels, rotary-dial phones were bolted to walls, and the only way to "google" something was to go to the local library.

In this century, the landscape has changed dramatically. Google, founded in 1998, got momentum around 2000. Facebook was founded in 2004, giving the entire world a common online social network. In 2006, Amazon.com essentially invented public cloud computing when it unveiled Amazon Web Services (AWS). Apple introduced the iPhone in 2007. Together those products and services laid the foundation for a new era driven by mobile devices, social networks, cloud computing, and data about everything. In the 2000s, Agile Software Development caught on, accelerating the ability to get new code out the door. New forms of financing such as crowd funding and angel investor networks coupled with the rise of start-up accelerators made it easier than ever to raise money for new companies, while at the same time the cost of everything involved in starting a tech company (aside from insanely expensive office space in Silicon Valley) fell through the floor. If in 2000 a new company would spend $1 million on technology to get a first viable product to market, by 2015 the cost to do the same had dropped to something like $10,000.[4] Meanwhile, a new generation of customers—Millennials, born since the 1980s— entered the market. They have lived their entire lives in the digital era and demand inexpensive, mobile, connected products and services. By 2020 this generation will make up half the workforce, driving business purchase decisions.

So starting a company and launching a product are cheaper and easier than any time in history, and that means that for every well-known problem, hundreds of solutions can instantly appear out of nowhere. Brand names you can't pronounce let alone remember pop up overnight. It's hard to know a Yik Yak from an itBit or a Nuzzel. The number of choices make it almost impossible to figure out which product to buy. Potential customers, whether they are consumers or enterprise buyers, easily wind up overwhelmed by the solutions pitched to them. It becomes much easier—much clearer—for people to think primarily in terms of the problem they want to solve. In that sense, a problem is a category. A company that best frames a problem is the company that often comes to define and take the category. Put another way: winning companies today market the problem, not just the solution.

For potential customers, categories become an organizing principle. The public comes to understand the problem that's been defined, and then demands a product or service that solves it. Uber initially built its new category around a simple, clear problem: taxi service usually sucks. As Uber expanded, it opened up more category potential by framing a broader problem: how can you reliably get around town without a car? Uber had to get people to understand that this was a problem that could be solved in a new, technology-based way. As often happens, it was a problem many people didn't know *could* be solved.

Once the public understands the problem, people latch on to the most popular solution. Given all of the product and service choices people must make, it can get too burdensome to research every offering. So we pick the leader. Global networks, search engines, and social media allow everyone to quickly identify the top solution. Almost as soon as the problem—the category—is well understood, customers find the most popular solution and flock to it. Especially for digital products and services, there is no reason for anyone to settle for what they see as second or third best. Everyone who wants the best can get the best, instantly. The perceived best takes almost all of the market share; second best manages to hold on to enough to keep going; and the rest get pretty much nothing.

The ideas behind categories and how customers organize their buying decisions have been understood for some time. Even in the 1970s, Ries and Trout described how, "[t]o cope with complexity,

people have learned to simplify everything." They added: "The rank-
ing of people, objects, and brands is not only a convenient method of
organizing things but also an absolute necessity to keep from being
overwhelmed by the complexities of life." (Amazing, right? People
in the seventies were overwhelmed! A real-life Austin Powers, frozen
since the sixties and revived in the 2010s, would blow his brain's
circuits by just walking into a Costco or looking at an iPhone App
Store.) And even back then, as Ries and Trout explained, marketers
knew that winning a category meant everything. "History shows
that the first brand into the brain gets twice the long-term market
share of the No. 2 brand and twice again as much as the No. 3
brand," they wrote. "And the relationships are not easily changed."[5]

What's different now, though, is the sheer magnitude and velocity of this dynamic. The 1970s saw, compared to today, few new
products or new categories because barriers to entry were so high.
New products—almost always physical in that nondigital age—had
to be manufactured and distributed. Getting the word out involved
buying costly advertising on TV or in print. Today, an offering like
Slack or Snapchat can be built by a handful of people in someone's basement and distributed globally through the cloud with one
mouse click. If people like it, it goes viral on social networks. No
need to buy $30 million Super Bowl ads. The complexity Ries and
Trout described has gone exponential, which makes the need to cat-
egorize more powerful than ever. Few people have the time or brain
capacity to make buying decisions any other way. So people look for
ways to make fewer choices in the face of more choices.[6] "Increased
choice among goods and services may contribute little or nothing to
the kind of freedom that counts," writes Barry Schwartz in *Paradox
of Choice*. "Indeed, it may impair freedom by taking time and energy
we'd be better off devoting to other matters."[7]

The category as an organizing principle is supported by research
on the brain and cognitive biases, as described by Nobel Prize
winner Daniel Kahneman in his book *Thinking, Fast and Slow*, and

by a host of brain scientists.[8] Our brains are governed by more than fifty different cognitive biases that push us toward decisions based not on facts and logic, but on instincts that can be at odds with facts and logic. It's a shortcut system in our brain—a way to make decisions faster and easier, especially when overwhelmed by too much information.

One of the cognitive biases is called the Anchoring Effect. It's a tendency for an early bit of information to affect our view of all the information that comes after. For instance, the first offer put on the table in a negotiation has a powerful impact on any other offer that comes after. So in category dynamics, an early company that solves the problem will win a powerful place in customers' minds. It becomes an anchor. Other companies coming afterward get judged against that early company. Another bias that kicks in is the Choice Supportive Bias—the tendency to give positive qualities to an option we've chosen just because we've chosen it. This means that once you've committed to a product or service in a new category, you're likely to feel certain that it is the best even if something slightly better comes along. This helps explain why category kings can't be dethroned by a competing product or service that's simply better. Once people have chosen a king, they will always tend to believe the king is better, even if it's not. This reality explains why companies with superior technology can still lose category wars. Once a king emerges customers believe it's the best, regardless of any evidence to the contrary.

The category king concept also plays out in humans' pack mentality. Groupthink Bias describes a tendency to believe things because other people do. Brain studies have shown that when we hold an opinion that differs from others' in a group, our brains produce an error signal, warning us that we are probably wrong. In a category, the Groupthink Bias brings momentum to an emerging category king—customers embrace the king because so many other customers have embraced the king. For some people the pressure to make important buying decisions is not unlike the feeling of being under threat. Research from Vladas Griskevicius at the University of Minnesota shows that when people are threatened they seek safety in numbers. "In the pack we feel less vulnerable, less likely to get eaten when the critter cannot see us because we blend in with the crowd. The group is our haven, our shield."[9] As a result, the people who already own iPads make the people thinking about buying iPads feel safer about the decision. The need to fit in is a uniquely human behavior and begins as early as two years old. "Conformity is a very basic feature of human sociality," said Daniel Haun, a psychological scientist at the Max Planck Institute for Evolutionary Anthropology.[10] Studies show that people will and do change their minds to fit in. MRI scans of people changing their minds to conform to a group show that two critical reward-related regions in our brain are stimulated when we change our minds to be like others. It turns out we want to buy from category kings because our brains feel safe and happy when we do.

Category thinking works because it's the way our brains work. More important, it's the mode of thinking that our brains turn to when faced with exactly the kind of overstimulated, crazy-ass marketplace we have today and will have in spades in coming years.

We further developed a link between a category-based strategy and brain science by studying market caps of public companies.

We analyzed the total value created by every technology IPO from 2000 to 2015, and found something remarkable.[11] We found a consistent "sweet spot" window. The data show that the best time for a company to go public is when it is between six and ten years old. Oracle, Cisco, Qualcomm, Google, VMware, and Red Hat are among the many enduring category kings that went public in the sweet spot window. Most of the companies that went public in the sweet spot are ones we'd identify as category kings.

We found that the age of a company at IPO even mattered more to post-IPO value creation than the amount invested in a company while it was still private. Seriously! There is zero correlation between the amount of money raised by a company before it goes public and its post-IPO value creation. The only consistent factor that mattered in our study was the age of the company. Huh?![12]

We got an aha when we looked at the research of Paul Geroski, author of *The Evolution of New Markets*. Geroski's research explains the stages in the evolution of a new market—that is, a new category. In a market's earliest stage, the number of companies (he calls them providers) in the space explodes. This is the phase when the new category is first defined and a gaggle of entrants are scrambling to solve the problem. In the middle phase, the number of companies dives as the king emerges and competitors disappear (because the king starts sucking up all the economics). In the last phase the number of companies bottoms out as the king dominates and reigns over the market. Inspired by his work, we created the category lifecycle model {figure 1}.

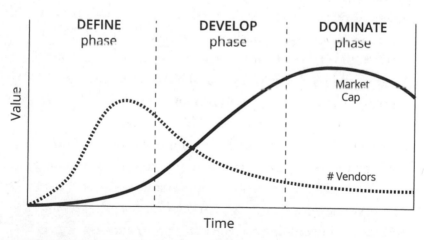

Adapted from: P.A. Geroski, "The Evolution of New Markets", Oxford University Press, 2009

Figure 1. The category lifecycle model shows the evolution of markets. As the market catches on, the total market cap of the companies in that market rises and the number of competitors falls. Category kings usually are solidified around the time those lines cross.

Now, as Geroski also showed, the market value of the whole category rises slowly in the first stage as a category gets on its feet, then like a rocket in the middle stage as the category catches on. In the last stage—the domination stage—value peaks and then tails off as the category matures.

Right in the middle of the category lifecycle model, the two lines—number of vendors and total category value—cross. Those lines cross when a category takes hold, a clear king emerges, the public understands the problem and solution, and investors pour money into the category and its king. It's the moment of category explosion.

Let's go back to our sweet spot research. We overlaid it on the category lifecycle model and saw that the sweet spot lands right around the moment Geroski's lines cross. That seems to show that the best time for a category-creating company to go public (our data) and the moment of category explosion are the same. And in the post-Internet era, that's consistently been about six to ten years after the first companies are founded in the category. We call this the 6–10 law. [Figure 2.] (Pre-Internet, categories took a little longer to spread throughout a market. In 1986, Microsoft went public in its sweet spot, and it was eleven years old.)

We ruminated until our heads hurt[13] looking for an explanation of why categories almost always take hold at about the same age.

Eventually, we circled back to brain science and cognitive biases. It takes a certain amount of time for people to shift their thinking and then change their buying behavior. Our brains can only accept a new problem and new solution so fast. The time it takes will be different depending on the scale of the problem. Certainly it's quicker for a teenager to discover Snapchat and change behavior around sending teenager stuff to friends than it is for a corporate IT chief to discover Salesforce.com and buy into a new way to run critical business operations. But that's why we see a span of six to ten years in the sweet spot. Simple consumer categories catch hold on the earlier side; complex enterprise categories

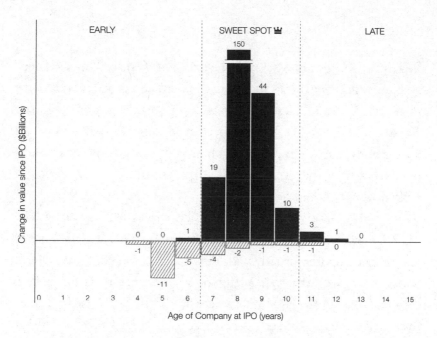

Figure 2. The 6–10 Law. The companies that create the most post-IPO value go public when they're around six to ten years old, and around the same time category kings typically win their crown.

take longer. But the absolutely essential point: It always takes time to define a category, develop it, and change the way we see a problem and its solution. And that time is measured in years.

What does all this mean for a CEO, founder, or category creator of any kind? Your number one job is to change the way people think. Your product, your company culture, your marketing—everything has to be aligned with transforming the way potential customers think. If you change the way they think, they will change their buying behavior. More important, if you are the company that changes the way people think, people will see your company as the category king, and you will win the majority of the customers.

That's why category is the new strategy.

And So: The Category Strategy

When Bill Gates ran Microsoft, he brilliantly created huge categories, most notably the PC operating system and office productivity suite. But Gates had a hard time seeing past his category-defining success, Windows. Oh, how he loved him some Windows. The old saying goes that when you have a hammer, everything looks like a nail, and Gates's hammer was Windows, so to him every problem looked like it should be solved using Windows.

In 2002, Gates unveiled what Microsoft called its Tablet PC. Now, by that time, lots of companies had made runs at some kind of tabletlike computer, usually with the idea that you could write on it with a stylus, as if you were jotting down notes in a meeting. In fact, for a few years in the late 1980s and early 1990s, "pen-based computing" made investors and engineers more excited than a teenage girl at a One Direction concert, certain as they were that this was the next big thing. Two pen computers, the GRiDPad and EO, made spectacular splashes. But those products were expensive and didn't do enough to be worthwhile. Nobody really understood what problem they solved. Before long, those early tablet computers disappeared.

But Gates believed in tablet computing and pushed development of a device at Microsoft. So confident was he in tablet computing, when he announced the Tablet PC he chirped, "Within five years, I predict it will be the most popular form of PC sold in America."

However, the Tablet PC ran Windows—the same Windows designed for laptops and desktops. Even the name "Tablet PC" gave away its genetic defect: it wasn't defining any new category, but instead was trying to be a PC in a slightly different form factor—a form factor that wasn't really suited for the kinds of things people usually did with PCs. Looking back a decade after the announcement, *Computerworld* magazine wrote: "Rather than envision what people would really want to do with a tablet and then design the hardware for that, Microsoft instead force-fit Windows XP onto it. Windows XP was a great desktop operating system, but it was bloated overkill for a tablet." Within five years, instead of flying off Best Buy shelves as Gates foretold, the Tablet PC was a goner. It failed to create or spark a new category.[14]

Eight years after Gates's announcement, Apple CEO Steve Jobs took the stage for one of his famously dramatic product unveilings. The room went dark, and Jobs put up a picture of an iPhone and a MacBook laptop, with a question mark in between. "Is there room for a third category of device in the middle?" Jobs said to the audience. He dismissed past efforts to fill that spot, saying they were just bad laptops. But, he said, there had to be a place in our lives for a device that is "so much more intimate than a laptop and so much more capable than a smartphone." With that, he showed the first iPad. And then Jobs uttered the magic words—the words that showed Apple had thought about this new product in a new way. The "iPad creates and defines an *entirely new category* of devices that will connect users with their apps and content in a much more intimate, intuitive and fun way than ever before."[15]

The iPad wasn't a laptop or a phone. It solved a new problem particular to the mobile-social-cloud era: people needed a device that they could carry around and use to watch videos, shop, read magazines, or muck around on Facebook. It didn't have to have the power and bulk of a laptop, but it did need a bigger screen than a smartphone. Jobs had identified a new problem, and developed a new kind of product to solve it. As he announced the iPad, Jobs made us see that we had this problem—even if we didn't think we did—and that Apple had the very best solution ever. Jobs intentionally, willfully, strategically created a new category and put the iPad at the top of it from day one. The product itself was not Apple's strategy. Selling more of a certain kind of software was not Apple's strategy. Creating the *category* was Apple's strategy.

Of course, it worked. In the first year, Apple sold about 15 million iPads, representing more than $10 billion in revenue. And soon after, copycat tablets showed up from competitors from around the world, including Samsung, LG, and eventually Microsoft. As almost always happens, though, the copycats barely impugned upon the category king's dominant share of the category's economics.[16]

Category as a strategy is not only for tech companies. Manoj Bhargava was born in India, moved to the United States when he was fourteen, dropped out of Princeton his freshman year, lived as a monk back in India for twelve years, moved back to the United States, then started a plastics company. In the early 2000s, as he wandered around a natural products trade show in Anaheim, California, Bhargava stopped at a booth selling a sixteen-ounce can of some liquid that was supposed to boost productivity for hours and tasted like absolute crap. "For the next six or seven hours, I was in great shape," the notably reclusive Bhargava told *Forbes* magazine. "I thought, wow, this is amazing. I can sell this." Yet he knew there was a reason these drinks hadn't caught on. At sixteen ounces, they were sold against other drinks such as Coca-Cola or Starbucks's Frappuccinos. Since energy drinks usually taste bad, they were mainly seen as bad drinks loaded with a ton of caffeine. "I thought, if I'm tired, am I also thirsty?" Bhargava said. "Is that like having a headache and a stomachache? It didn't make any sense."[17]

Bhargava saw an opening for a new category: the energy shot. It would be something that hadn't existed before, sold not against drinks but on its own, near the cash register in stores. In six months he came up with a concentration of caffeine and B vitamins that he could package in a tiny red two-ounce bottle. The brand name was straightforward: 5-hour Energy. It broke through by solving a clear problem in a new way. The problem was that people got tired and needed a boost to study or work or drive. The new solution was one quick shot that would provide that boost for five hours, without making you drink a whole can of awful. In a crowded market of drinks and caffeinated potions, Bhargava created, then developed and dominated a brand-new category. By

2011, 5-hour Energy hit $1 billion in sales, and the company commanded 90 percent of the energy shot category. Bhargava became a billionaire—and committed 90 percent of his earnings to charity. Much like Apple with its iPad, the category was Bhargava's strategy. He envisioned the category and how to build it, evangelized the problem, then created the product and company to attack it.

A lot of venture capitalists like to say, "We invest in great teams." But a great team is nothing without a great category. A great team in a lousy category or a me-too position in an existing category is a losing cause. But if a middling team stumbles on a great category, the category will make heroes of the team. The product doesn't have to be an engineering marvel, either—it just has to be good enough to satisfy the category.

When the right product and right company connect to a strong category, the category literally pulls the product or service out of the company. We see that all the time with these rocketing start-ups, from Facebook in the early 2000s to Slack in the mid-2010s. Once the category's problem gets defined, the market demands the solution, and potential customers will turn to the consensus solution with ferocity. In a well-honed category-driven strategy, the company designs the category, evangelizes the problem, offers its solution to the problem, and then *the category makes the company its king.* The greatest power comes from the people proclaiming their own king. A self-determined king that isn't made by the category is a hollow despot destined to be overthrown at the first sign of weakness.

This is why a category-based strategy requires the design of a great product, a great company, and a great category at roughly the same time. They are of a piece—designed to work together to change the way people think. We depict the strategy as a triangle, with each side of equal importance. (Actually, we prefer to think of it as a bar stool with three legs required to keep us firmly seated in front of our beers, but a triangle is easier to draw.) Category-driven strategy looks like this [Figure 3]:

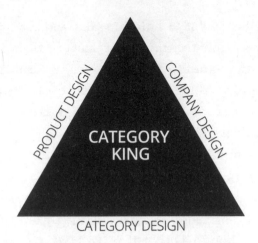

Figure 3. The magic triangle: to improve the odds of becoming a category king, companies should engage in product design, company design, and category design at roughly the same time.

Product design is the purposeful building of a product and experience that solves the problem the market needs solved. The goal is what is traditionally called a great product/market fit—in other words, a great product/category fit. In the tech start-up world, most companies actually begin with a product—a couple of folks messing around in a garage to make something.

Company design is the purposeful creation of a business model and an organization with a culture and point of view that fits with the category. The goal is a great company/category fit.

Category design is the mindful creation and development of a new market category, designed so the category will pull in customers who will then make the company its king. In marketing terms it's "the air wars." It's about winning the war for popular opinion, teaching the world to abandon the old and embrace the new. Category design builds the profile of the space while drawing attention to the company creating it. The next chapter will go into a deeper exploration of category design.

All three elements—company design, product design, and category design—work together and balance each other to exert great force on a company's success and value. The legendary, enduring companies get the three elements of company design, product design, and category design in such a state of synchronicity, they reinforce each other and build momentum in a flywheel effect. We'll discuss the flywheel in greater detail in chapter 8.

The triangle of design might look like it is specific to start-up companies, but that's not the only way it works. Enduring companies that build powerful flywheels create and expand categories over and over. As we'll get to later in the book, Amazon.com has been a master at creating new categories at the same time as it creates a new product while also making sure the company fits the category. It did this with the Kindle e-reader and with Amazon Web Services cloud computing. Corning has pulled off this kind of strategy over and over for 165 years, and is still doing it today with new categories of glass that never before existed. One of the greatest category creation events in computing history was orchestrated by IBM when it brought out its System/360 computer in 1964, more than fifty years after the company was founded.

The triangle can work in more circumscribed ways, too. Every department inside a larger business is essentially creating a product or service of some kind, and would benefit from thinking about the category it serves and how the department and its offering plug into that category. Individuals can think this way about their careers. The most successful people identify a category, an offering (what they can uniquely do that the category needs), and a personal culture and point of view (who they are and how they think) at the same time. Muhammad Ali created a category of showman-boxer, perfectly suited to the emerging age of television, that hadn't existed before. The category reflected what he could do and how he thought, and he completely dominated it for the rest of his career. No one else emerged who could compete with him. Harry Potter author J. K. Rowling did the same, inventing an intellectual young-adult fiction category and making herself the category king. The principles of category thinking also apply to the kinds of people at the office who build their careers by successfully developing a niche and putting themselves at the top of it.

Google, Through a Category Lens

Few companies start on day one with all three points of the triangle firmly planned out. Some companies begin with a team that just wants to work together, essentially beginning with company design. Some companies get their start because an entrepreneur thinks up a new product, starting at product design. And some companies begin with a vision for a category—like Bhargava of 5-hour Energy, who then had to design a product and company to tackle the category. Still, legendary companies quickly move past their initial impetus and grasp category thinking, embracing all three points of the triangle. However they start, these companies quickly move to designing the product, company, and category in parallel.

With that in mind, we want to tell you the story of Google in a way you probably hadn't considered. A lot of people think Google was just a *better* search engine when it appeared in 2000. Even Google had bought into the classic engineering conceit that echoes the *Field of Dreams* mantra, "If you build it, they will come." Just make a great product and people will find it. That kind of thinking makes it hard to understand why Google became such a juggernaut even though a bunch of reasonably popular search engines already existed. If it was just a better product in an existing category, how did it become a category king?

But there's another, revealing way to look at Google's success.

Before Google, all sorts of search engines proliferated: Alta Vista, Lycos, Infoseek, Ask Jeeves, AllTheWeb, and more. They seemed awesome at the time because nothing like a search engine had ever existed. But none of those search engines made real money—the only way they could monetize search was through banner ads, which never worked well for anybody. None of them broke out from the pack and led the market. They all worked off a similar idea: their software crawled through the words on Web pages to find matches with the words users typed in. That process, though, meant that you got a lot of shitty results just because a word you typed appeared a few times in some document. Searching by keyword also meant that the bigger the Web got, the slower the search engines got, since the search engine computers had to crawl through an exploding volume of pages.

In their dorm rooms at Stanford University at the end of the 1990s, Larry Page and Sergey Brin came up with a *different* insight—a technology insight. They realized they could use the links between pages on the nascent World Wide Web to rank pages and websites, counting links similar to the way you might count votes. More links to a page were like more votes that the page was worthwhile. This method tended to push higher-quality results to the top, plus the system also got better as the Web grew, learning from the links and from the search activity of users. More Web pages meant more votes, and more votes produced results that weren't just better—Google's results often seemed prescient, seeming to understand what you were actually looking for.[18] Google was the kind of innovation only someone outside of traditional search and computer science could've come up with. "The whole field had suffered blinders," Bell Labs computer scientist Amit Singhal said at the time. "Search really did need two people who were never tainted by people like me to come up with that shake-up."[19]

So Google wasn't just another search engine—Google created a new *category* of search that drew power from the very structure of the burgeoning Web. Google from the start was something different, not just better. It solved a clear problem for its users who wanted spot-on results from an ever more chaotic Web. It redefined the very meaning of "search" on the Web and of course became a verb: *to google*. And once the public realized Google was solving a problem they were newly made aware of (remember, we thought Alta Vista's results were amazing at first), the new category exerted massive pull on Google. People pulled the product to them in exploding numbers, even though Google did almost no marketing or messaging to develop the category at first. It didn't even know it had created a category.

However, imagine if Google had never done anything else— imagine it only understood itself as a better search engine. Google would not be the powerhouse it is today. It would've just been a great product, and maybe Microsoft would've bought it to get Google's technology, saving itself from its eventual Bing doltishness. But instead, Page and Brin pretty quickly found a way to monetize this new search paradigm with a new search advertising paradigm, creating AdWords. For the first time, ads could be matched to search terms, and advertisers could pay for an ad's performance instead of paying for random "eyeballs" seeing an ad. As part of this revolution in advertising, Google reimagined how advertisers would purchase ads—by bidding, auction-style, on search terms. Google brilliantly changed the advertising business model, coupling it with a particularly powerful characteristic of search: when you search for something, you tell Google a little about yourself at that moment in time, and that's a lot more than most advertisers ever had before. At that point, Page and Brin were birthing a category that was truly revolutionary—a swizzle of very personal information services and advertising—and they evangelized it to advertisers.

It was so powerful and new, the money started flooding in to Google, and the company used this cash flow to extend and extend and extend its category by creating more information services that would tell advertisers something about the target consumer at that moment. Google Maps reveals where you are, Gmail sees

what you're writing about, Calendar has your schedule, Google
Docs can glimpse what you're working on. The company bought
YouTube so it could know what you're watching. It built Android
so it could take that whole search-advertising stew into mobile
phones. Google started with a search product that was different,
and then redefined "search" into something much, much bigger
and different than it had meant before, funded by an entirely
new category of advertising. Though we are not sure Google ever
understood it this way, it had embarked on a brilliant category
strategy—the kind we'll unpack as we go through this book.[20]
As a result, Google has transformed the way we get and consume
information, reinvented advertising, created more than fifty thousand high-value jobs, and built an ecosystem of partners who've
built huge businesses around Google's category.

By the mid-2000s, Google's competition in search was either gone or neutered. In mid-2015, according to research firm
StatCounter, Google search commanded a 74.8 percent market
share, while Bing had 12.4 percent, followed by Yahoo (which
built its own search engine in 2003) at 10.9 percent. All signs
point to Google as one of the great category kings of all time.
Whether Google knew what it was doing or not, it put together
the three parts of the triangle. Conventional wisdom says Google
won simply because it built a better search engine. But it won
because it also designed a new category and designed its company to fit that category.

So no matter where you start on the triangle of category thinking, ultimately category design can't be left to chance. A great
product and great company are nothing without a great category.
The company that leaves category design to someone else is tempting fate, potentially wasting the opportunity to be a category
king. And as we've seen, the king takes almost all of the category's
economics—market share, market cap, and profits—leaving its
followers with crumbs.

A Category Crowns a King

We love Diane Greene, founding CEO of VMware, and think she's brilliant. We talked to her about VMware's beginnings, and came to realize that at the start, VMware had no idea it was about to create a powerful category.

The VMware product started as a research project by Greene's husband, Mendel Rosenblum, a computer science professor at Stanford. At the time, computers could run a single operating system, like Microsoft's Windows. Rosenblum developed software that would essentially partition a computer, allowing it to run another operating system at the same time. The second operating system would be kind of a virtual computer running inside another computer, so Greene and Rosenblum started calling their product "virtualization software." At first, the product was aimed at researchers who might want to run an experimental piece of software in a safe container inside a computer, avoiding the risk of the experimental software fucking up everything else on the machine. "Our early customers were all physics and chemistry professors," Greene told us. "It was our internal joke: 'VMware—it's not for everybody. You have to be really smart.'"[21]

Still, Greene and Rosenblum weren't naive. They realized they'd created a new kind of product, and that it could be useful in a lot of situations—like for corporations wanting to safely test software on their systems. So in 1998 they started a company, made Greene CEO, and shortened "virtual machine software" to VMware—a name pretty much everybody involved hated. They found that the technology was difficult to explain. A lot of venture capitalists didn't invest because they didn't understand the market—in part because Greene didn't even understand the market. "We didn't think it was going to become a multibillion-dollar industry," she told us. "We just said, 'This is, like, really needed.'"

VMware's founders started at the product design corner of the triangle. They knew that technologists had at least a vague sense they needed virtualization software. Greene was still struggling to comprehend and articulate the category when VMware was ready to release the first version of its product. Instead of trying to sell the software through typical channels, Greene decided to put it up on VMware's website and allow people to use it for free for thirty days. VMware posted the software on a Sunday afternoon.

"We only had a limited amount of bandwidth that we had paid for," Greene recalled. "And so we came in at like six in the morning [on Monday], and there's all these emails from this kid at Cornell, and he goes, 'VMware—your site went away. It ran out of bandwidth. I'm hosting it at Cornell and I'll record everybody that comes and share all that information with you.'" When Greene and her team looked, 75,000 people had downloaded the product.

It dawned on Greene that VMware had created an entirely new category—virtual machine software—that had fantastic potential. She dove into a version of category design, talking to the media about how this new product worked and how it could save corporations fantastic amounts of money on operating their computer systems. She realized there was a huge problem VMware could solve—vastly underutilized corporate computers—and started to publicize it. Another smart move: "Right away, we devised a huge training program, where you could become VMware certified," she said. It was a tactic for shaping the category and building an ecosystem of users and believers. Over the next few years, Greene did a lot of things right to design and develop this category and ensure that VMware was its undisputed king. But the important part of this story is the way the category instantly embraced VMware and *made* it the king. The category, once born, was so grateful to VMware for designing a product and company that could serve it, the category pulled VMware out of obscurity and practically carried it to a throne. By giving the category definition, the category arose out of nothing, and a new king was born. VMware, by the way, went public nine years after it was founded and created the category, fitting with our 6–10 Law.

A lesson here is that a category needs a king. New categories benefit from a near monopoly. When we don't yet know where a category is going or what it can become, we really want a king to take charge, set the rules, and define the category. We really want a king to step up and give us a clear choice that we can commit to. A category stalls when that doesn't happen. In capitalist societies, there's a stubborn conviction that intense competition is always better for the public: the harder firms compete, the more efficient and innovative they become, driving down prices and giving us cooler products and services. But that's usually only true in mature businesses, where the categories have been around forever. Frozen foods needed Birds Eye to develop the category, but now the category is mature and the problem it once represented is thoroughly defined and solved. The category no longer needs a visionary leader to bring it to life. All that's left to accomplish are incremental improvements in price and quality, and competition is good at driving that. Looked at another way, if Birds Eye had a near monopoly on frozen foods for nearly a hundred years, we'd now be paying a lot more for frozen food that hasn't improved much in decades. Over time, monopolies tend to get lazy and greedy. But in the category-building stage, a strong king makes all the difference.

Finally, as we alluded to earlier, new technology has made it possible to create categories faster than ever. Speed as a competitive weapon has always mattered, especially in technology. Entrepreneurs, CEOs, and VCs have put their faith in speed-based strategies like "first-mover advantage" for decades. But in the mobile-social-cloud era, companies have no time to waste in adopting category thinking. We believe this trend will hold true in good times or bad. It certainly has in the past—our window for analyzing start-up data included both terrible times for tech investment (2000–2001, right after the dot-com crash, and 2008–09, after financial markets melted down) and exuberant times (2004–07, 2011–15). The trend toward speed holds up through all these eras.

What does this mean for entrepreneurs, CEOs, executives, investors, and other go-getters? You have no time to waste! So read this book as fast as you can, then get to work on your category.

3

The Discipline of Category Design

Great Category Design in World History

37 AD to 67 AD: Apostle Paul journeys through the known civilized world, conditioning the market and designing a new category of religion based on Jesus Christ's teachings about love and forgiveness.

1776: Rebels in the English colonies in America sign the Declaration of Independence, designing a new category of nation based on democracy and equality.

1848: Karl Marx and Friedrich Engels publish *The Communist Manifesto*, which Vladimir Lenin uses to design a new (and ultimately flawed) category of nation dominated by poor and struggling proletarians.

1912: Hawaiian-born Duke Paoa Kahinu Mokoe Hulikohola Kahanamoku begins traveling the world giving surfing exhibitions and designing a new category of sport that six decades later will help Al get girls in Australia.

1964: *Meet the Beatles* conditions the market for intelligent pop-rock, a once-dominant but currently dormant category.

1999: Salesforce.com's "No Software" campaign conditions the market to desire a new category of cloud-based applications. In doing so, CEO Marc Benioff exemplifies modern category design.

What the Hell Is Category Design?

Let's point the lens at ourselves: what problem is category design solving?

The problem, at its core, is that very few people are walking around with the equivalent of Steve Jobs's intuition. Too many good companies with good products fail to make a dent in the universe[1]—because they can't find their place in the universe. Too many companies essentially stick a pole in the air during a thunderstorm and hope they get struck by lightning. Entrepreneurs have an "aha" that compels them to solve a problem. Category designers take the next step to condition the market to see their aha the way they do and demand the new thing. The odds of success in this fast-moving, highly networked era are too overwhelming unless you possess the extremely rare talent of Jobs or one of the other preternaturally brilliant category designers such as Marc Benioff or Jeff Bezos. For every other smart, ambitious person, category design can provide a systematic approach to improving the odds of becoming a category king—of finding a way to play bigger.

And category design combined with company design and product design is the way to change how people think, and so change their buying behavior.

We are players turned coaches, and in our playing days we felt what it's like when there was no category design in place— when no sense of meaning and direction lashed together all of a team's work in a concerted effort to dent the universe. Maybe it's happening in your company now. You feel it when the chief marketing officer presents new branding that looks like a bad face tattoo that you'll regret in a year, or when the sales staff demands more case studies because they can't figure out how to win deals, or engineers build product by adding every feature customers ask for—a sure and probably disastrous indication that a company is letting its customers design its category. (As Henry Ford famously-supposedly said: "If I had asked people what they wanted, they would have said faster horses.") You feel the absence of category design when you hire McKinsey to do another study that will cost a gazillion fucking dollars or when investment bankers pitch acquisitions that make as much sense as adding chocolate syrup to beer. You feel it when a Gartner Magic Quadrant gets published and you're lost in the bottom part of the chart, or when you get an RFP from a Fortune 500 company that was clearly written by one of your competitors. You feel it when you and a lot of smart people on your team are earnestly doing their jobs, putting in long hours and trying really hard, and little of it seems to get traction. At one time or another, each of us writing this book has experienced some or all of these things, and to put it bluntly: it feels like ass.

We've spent our whole careers trying to understand category king thinking and category design, and now we believe it's time to develop a new *discipline* called category design. We've been trying to solve this problem for two decades, collectively and individually. We've lived the process of category creation, studied the great category designers, and analyzed data on every tech company founded since 2000 to get insights into the dynamics of creating new categories. We also know how important it can be to create a new discipline at the moment in time when it's needed—because we've done it before.

This is how a new discipline happens:

In the early 2000s, all three of us were working with the leadership team at Macromedia, which became most famous for making the Flash software that brought video to the Internet masses. Macromedia's CEO was Rob Burgess, and he was looking over the company's hodgepodge of products, and said to us, "I've got a bag of doorknobs.[2] I keep adding to the doorknobs, and the revenue doesn't move. We need to drive growth, so help me figure something out."

The three of us were asked to help Macromedia explain its unique place in the tech universe and to reposition the company.

We brought a lot of collective experience to this problem. Al's first entrepreneurial stint involved pioneering a new space in UNIX systems management during the 1980s. As CEO of Quokka Sports during the dot-com boom of the 1990s, he created a new category called sports immersion at the intersection of sports, data, and Internet content. Christopher was among the first to evangelize what became the customer relationship management (CRM) category, landing him the top marketing job at Vantive in Silicon Valley. Then as the Internet was ascending, he helped build Scient, a firm committed to dominating a new space of "eBusiness," back when eBusiness seemed like a new idea. Dave cut his teeth as a category marketer working with Christopher at Vantive, and then went on to work at creating new spaces in sales configuration software and, as mentioned earlier, Internet talk radio. By the time Dave, Al, and Christopher worked together for Macromedia, each had developed and tested approaches to creating new categories. Many of these ideas informed our later practice at Play Bigger and are reflected in this book.

As the three of us worked through Macromedia's situation with our category-thinking caps on, we zeroed in on the importance of "experience" in the emerging digital economy. The Internet made it so easy to click from one website to another, it had created a new problem: sites found it difficult to keep people engaged. So we saw a new problem that Macromedia could solve. Macromedia could help sites become more "sticky" by improving the quality of the experience on the site. Seems so obvious now, but at the time this counted as a revelation.

Macromedia, we urged, had to become known for products that help Web developers and designers deliver great experiences for users. This was not just about the engineering that would go into products—it meant understanding the context around users when they touched experiences that were created using Macro-media products. It meant understanding how the products and the branding and the customer service and everything else made people feel, and designing the experience so it made them feel good. A term surfaced out of all this thinking: *experience design*.

Now, there is a long history of new disciplines emerging in business and technology. In the early twentieth century, mech-anization and electricity introduced complex products to busi-nesses and consumers—things like cars, washing machines, toasters, punch-card tabulating machines (the first computers), and farm machines. A new problem manifested itself: how to make the machinery attractive and usable for a wide audience. By the 1920s, a new discipline emerged to solve that problem, and it was called industrial design. This profession "within a de-cade changed American products from mechanical monstrosities into sleek, modern forms expressive of the future," wrote Carroll Gantz, author of *Founders of American Industrial Design*.[3] Then, in the 1980s, computer technology for the first time started mak-ing its way to mass markets, and that presented a problem that industrial design wasn't solving: how to help humans interact and connect with digital devices. Again, a new discipline arose to solve the new problem. Gestated at Stanford University and birthed at IDEO, it became known as product design, meshing the art of design with engineering. By applying that discipline, IDEO designed the first mouse for a commercial PC and the first commercial laptop. Product design is a given in technology today—no company would *not* do it. "We used to think product design was a really goofy program, kind of at the outskirts of engineering in some far-off building," Dennis Boyle, an IDEO founder, told us, reflecting on the history of the discipline. "Now it's much more front-and-center, which is lovely."[4]

History, then, suggests that a time of transition calls for a new discipline that helps shape and tame the new forces for the rest of us. Industrial designers did that for mechanization. Product designers did that for computerization.

Sitting inside Macromedia, we realized that the Internet had unleashed another transition that required a discipline to help humans interact with online products and services. And experience design has evolved to become part of the fabric of the technology industry. No right-minded company today would *not* do it.

At Macromedia, experience design brought together many seemingly disparate functions, including visual design, user experience (known as UX), product management and development, branding, and marketing. Macromedia concluded that it needed to take the lead in experience design and become known for it. And from that, a company tagline emerged: "Experience Matters." Macromedia used experience design to invent a new category that it called Rich Internet Applications, which delivered multimedia to users, and the company packaged its disparate "doorknobs" into Macromedia Studio MX. Those products fundamentally transformed the company, its position, and its revenue. In 2005, Adobe bought Macromedia for $3.4 billion. A big part of that valuation came from Macromedia's "Experience Matters" position atop the Rich Internet Applications category it had invented.

When we chose to hang up our skates as players and make the transition to coaches, we began coupling our personal experiences with research and data science analysis to try to hack the code on how to build category king companies. As we put all of this together, it became apparent that today's mobile-social-cloud, ultra-networked, always-on era has whipped up yet another transition, but this time it's for companies themselves. The transition has created a new set of problems, which we laid out earlier—including how to solve for winner-take-all markets and increasing noise from floods of start-ups. We believe that a discipline needs to arise to tame modern forces and increase the odds of success. We propose that it is category design.

We believe we've landed on insights and ideas worthy of consideration by entrepreneurs, investors, managers, and ambitious people who want to leave that dent in the universe. We created category design as a disciplined approach to taking the intrinsic nature of the greatest entrepreneurial successes and making it explicit. We by no means are saying we figured it all out. As guys who've spent about thirty years each in the tech business, we think we're just scratching the surface. It is our hope that you will take what we've uncovered through analysis, research, and experience and use it as a starting point for your own thinking. Our goal is to stoke a conversation about how to increase the odds for people who want to build a legendary category and company.

At least category design is a better plan than saying you're either Steve Jobs or you hope to get hit by lightning. Dumb luck is not a viable strategy.

Okay, but Hold On— What the Hell Is Category Design?

Category design is the discipline of creating and developing a new market category, and conditioning the market so it will demand your solution and crown your company as its king.

Category design means bringing together many activities across your company and executing on the tactics described in this book. It is a discipline and a future career. Just as someone can be a product designer or experience designer, there will be a role at many companies for a category designer. And like experience or product design, there will be a leader who takes responsibility for bringing it all together to give the company the best chance of becoming category king.

Key traits of category design, which we'll unpack in coming chapters:

- Category design drives the company's strategy to become a category king. The strategy has to start with the CEO and her leadership team identifying the right category to create, making sure the product and company fit the category.
- Category design involves product and ecosystem design. That includes creating a blueprint that generates a belief that you have the solution to an urgent and giant problem. It means developing an environment around your product that wins loyalty and gratitude for the product and company. When you have tens of thousands of people attending an event like Salesforce.com's Dreamforce, Facebook's F8, or VMware's VMworld, you know you sit atop a powerful category ecosystem.
- Category design is part of company culture. It is directly connected to the kind of company you build, the type of people you hire, and the type of community around the company including investors, partners, analysts, and journalists. It is the company's point of view on the world.
- Category design is about creating a powerful and provocative story that causes customers or users to make a choice. The story evokes something different from what came before, not just better.
- Category design is marketing, public relations, and advertising when it is all focused on conditioning the market to desire and need whatever you're giving it. The goal is to condition the market to have an *aha* that changes people's consumption, usage, and buying decisions. This is much more than messaging and branding.
- Above all, category design is making all of these components work together, in lockstep, feeding off each other, so each action builds momentum for the category and its king. In that sense, category design is like a musical score for a symphony.

Just as every part of the orchestra needs to play the score together, every part of the company needs to execute category
design together.

Maybe at this point you're thinking, "This sounds like a lot of
work! I just want to build this little app that does this cool little
thing and get it out there!" But category design is about increasing the odds that your work matters. Too many CEOs believe that
customers will buy when they learn about the features of their
breakthrough innovation. But a product and a company don't
float in space. A product and a company exist inside a category. If
you don't take charge of the category, someone else will, and then
you're royally screwed. Position yourself or be positioned.

Another mistake would be assuming that the space around the
company is outside of your control. Some executives talk about the
market like it's the weather—something that happens to them,
versus something that they can affect and in some cases even control. But here's the key: if you're creating a *new* category, you can
make the kind of weather you want to live in. If you move into
someone else's category, you certainly can't do much about the conditions around your company. If you open up a new category or
define the rules for an emerging one, you get to design the whole
space the way you want it.

But remember: *you have to design it*! If you leave design to chance,
someone else will design it—maybe a competitor, maybe customers, maybe a Gartner Group analyst, maybe the press. But if it's
not you, that means you blew a golden opportunity to increase
your odds of success.

Engineering schools teach that good technology will always
win. Tech companies can now get product out so quickly and
cheaply, it's tempting to rush right by category design. Getting
a product out can trump even considering the larger space, so
many won't think about the category because it's hard and because

category design can't be measured instantly. And then when a great product fails, the team believes they ran into bad luck. But to again invoke poker champion Greg Raymer, the odds are the same for everyone in the game. The key is to play bigger by doing everything in your power to increase *your* odds. It won't guarantee winning, but it gives you a better chance than others around you—and certainly a better chance than hoping to get struck by lightning. Category design is the twenty-first-century way to increase your odds.

The Ol' Frotos: How to Think About Category Design

Category design takes people on a journey. We refer to it as creating a from/to. Actually, we use a shorthand term: *frotos*. Remember, a great new category is one that solves a problem people didn't know they had, or solves an obvious problem no one thought could be solved. Either way, you are introducing something new to potential customers' lives. You have to help them move *from* the way they used to think, *to* a new frame of reference. This is what it means to condition the market. You have to first define and market the problem—and only then can you help people understand that you can solve the problem better than anyone else. VMware had to make technologists feel that an inability to run two or more operating systems on a computer was a problem. Before VMware, that problem didn't exist in the heads of most computer operators. As it happened, as soon as VMware revealed the problem, technologists immediately got it and felt a critical need to solve the problem. At that point, VMware was the perceived leader, and customers pulled the product right out of VMware. Likewise, Google had to make us realize that Alta Vista's search results were a problem. Uber had to get us to understand that hailing a taxi sucked and there was a better way. Defining the problem is the start of a journey, and it has to ring true to everyone in the company's orbit—customers, employees, investors, outside developers, partners, bloggers, and journalists. Everyone starts at *from*. You have to make sure they get to your *to*.

Marc Benioff taught everyone in the tech industry a lot about how to do that. We've followed the founder and CEO of Salesforce .com for a long time. Kevin has been interviewing him for stories and columns since the company's founding in 1999, and Christopher and Dave were at Vantive in the mid-1990s, working in the technology space that Salesforce eventually usurped. From our perspective, Benioff pulled off one of the model category design strategies of our era. He conditioned the market to accept his vision.

First of all, consider the *from* to at the time. In 1999, "cloud computing" was a foreign phrase. Convincing a chief technology officer to rely on cloud computing in 1999 would've been like trying to persuade someone to open a sushi joint in Oklahoma in 1950. Amazon Web Services, which created the category of public cloud computing, wouldn't launch until 2006—and even then, Amazon CEO Jeff Bezos struggled to describe and explain his new service.[5] No corporation wanted to put its data on some dot-com company's computers. When a corporation in the 1990s needed software to help run its business, it bought and installed expensive, complex programs on its own computer systems. One red-hot category of corporate software at the time was called CRM—customer relationship management. It helped a salesforce track customers and prospects, coordinate sales activity, and share helpful information. And the red-hot category king selling this expensive, complex CRM software was Siebel Systems—cofounded (along with Patricia House) in 1993 by Thomas Siebel, who previously worked as a top executive at Oracle, where Benioff was a fast-rising star. Siebel and Benioff knew each other well at Oracle.[6]

So the *from* at the time was Siebel's CRM software, which corporations thought would solve a problem they'd had for a long time—the problem of how to automate sales activity. But while still at Oracle, even as Siebel soared in the CRM space, Benioff recognized a new problem with CRM that he thought he could solve: Siebel software was so expensive and complex it often frustrated customers who tried to implement it or scared companies away from buying it in the first place.

In the emerging Internet, Benioff envisioned a solution to the problem. He could put CRM-style software in one central data center, and let customers use the application through the Internet. Instead of charging millions of dollars up front for the software, he could charge a more affordable subscription fee. Instead of requiring the corporate customer to employ IT people to maintain the complex software on the company's own machines, Benioff could take care of the software in its data center, so customers would never have to touch it. Benioff left Oracle to start Salesforce.com and market a product that would be cheaper and easier to use than Siebel's—but most important, it would be different. It was also, at that moment in time, tremendously nonconsensus. Most corporate IT people looked at Salesforce in its early days and said: it'll never work.

Benioff didn't leave the category to chance. He didn't just believe the cool new product would sell itself. He understood that to get funding, hire employees, and win customers, he had to take the world on a journey. He had to condition the market.

In 1999, he started doing that while Salesforce was still only a few coders working in a San Francisco apartment. Benioff invited Don Clark, a reporter for the *Wall Street Journal*, to visit, but Benioff didn't spend time selling his solution. He evangelized the problem. On July 21, 1999, the *Journal* ran Clark's story on the front page. Headlined "Canceled Programs: Software Is Becoming an Online Service, Shaking Up an Industry," the story marked a first step in conditioning the market to desire what Salesforce would eventually give it. Benioff followed up that publicity by talking to other journalists and throwing launch parties under the theme "The End of Software." The phrase would become Salesforce's mantra. The company even designed a clever "No Software!" logo that mirrored the old *Ghostbusters* movie logo. Notice that there is nothing about Salesforce itself in those slogans and logos. Benioff's first priority was creating a category. He focused on defining the problem only he could solve. "We needed to introduce an entirely new market and promote a new way of doing business," Benioff recounted in his book, *Behind the Cloud.*[7]

From there Benioff got creative, and he used Siebel as his foil. Siebel was a tangible example of the problem Benioff needed to define. So he positioned Salesforce as the anti-Siebel. He wanted his company to be seen as the pirates storming Siebel's fortress. "We applied for a permit from the city [of San Francisco] to march against software," he told the *New York Times* a few years later. "We claimed it was hurting the American economy. It was creating landfills full of CD-ROMs. And the city granted it to us!"[8] Benioff led a tongue-in-cheek antisoftware protest.

Unlike so many excruciatingly diplomatic CEOs, Benioff publicly taunted his much bigger competitors, especially Siebel Systems and SAP, which also sold a CRM system.[9] He sounded at times like he was blowing more smoke than Foghorn Leghorn in a Looney Toons short. ("I say, I say, pay attention, boy, and you might learn somethin' about the future of software.") But to him, the effort and grandstanding were all about laying the groundwork for this new category, and positioning Salesforce as the company that could solve the problem and lead the world to a new vision.[10]

As journalists, analysts, and potential customers woke up to this new problem, Siebel felt like it had to react, even though Salesforce at that time posed little threat to Siebel's economics. "As [Siebel] began defending itself and acknowledging Salesforce .com," Benioff wrote, "the press began to see this fight as an increasingly interesting story, and that further legitimized us. At this point, we had already won."[11] Salesforce won because once people can see the problem, they can't unsee it. In a flash, Siebel had been labeled as a problem. Salesforce positioned itself as the solution. Benioff created the perception that Salesforce's category kingship was inevitable. From nothing, his vision became a self-fulfilling prophecy.

Of course, Salesforce then had to deliver. It had to actually build the technology to adequately solve the problem. But when the category demands a product, the product doesn't have to be perfect right from the get-go. Once the cloud-based sales-force automation category revealed the problem, the market demanded any viable solution. Since Salesforce set up the problem and defined its parameters, it stood at the beginning as the only viable solution. The market looked at Salesforce and said, Give us what you've got! Now, dammit!

Benioff also successfully imbued Salesforce with a strong point of view and persona. The company was the pirate, the radical visionary, the outsider (even though Benioff, the Oracle prodigy, was very much an insider in the software business!). The company infected customers and developers with its point of view. Work with us, Salesforce said, and show those establishment pigs how to do things. Benioff linked himself to the Dalai Lama, invoking a spiritual leader who rejects materialism—as if Benioff were a rebel among Porsche-driving CEO narcissists. That led to a moment of international notoriety in the early 2000s when Salesforce put out a promotional poster of the Dalai Lama appearing to endorse the company. An uproar followed. Benioff apologized. The incident blew over. Salesforce was left better known than if the incident had never happened at all. (Now *that* is one classic hijack—a tactic we'll get into later.) In perhaps his most inspired insult to the established CRM industry, Benioff chose as his company's New York Stock Exchange symbol "CRM."

By the time Salesforce went public in 2004, it had signed up

10,000 customers and nearly 140,000 users, each paying $65 to $125 a month for the service.[12] Siebel was on the defensive and tried to introduce a competing cloud-based subscription product, CRM OnDemand, but by then Salesforce was the emerging category king of cloud-based sales-force automation. The category had made Salesforce its king, and in that category, Siebel found it was the me-too wannabe. Even worse for Siebel, as Benioff recalled, "By getting behind this [cloud software], they've validated the market for us." Salesforce.com had effectively designed its category so the category crowned Salesforce as its king. Siebel entered the category and had to play by Salesforce's rules, and so its defeat was certain. The company that defines the space is best positioned to dominate it.

It's important to note that Salesforce did not disrupt Siebel. It created a new category that Siebel couldn't play in. The new category made people see a problem with the old category, so some of Siebel's customers migrated to the new one—yet a huge number of Salesforce's customers were newcomers to sales-force automation, unable to afford or implement the older CRM software. Siebel may have still dominated its old category, but Salesforce's new category sucked the vitality out of Siebel's old one. This may seem like semantics, but it's a matter of cause and effect: you don't first disrupt and then create the new—you create the new, and if that disrupts the old, so be it.

In September 2005, Oracle agreed to buy an injured Siebel for $5.8 billion. In early 2015, Salesforce.com's market cap was about $48 billion, and it employed 16,000 people. Its annual Dreamforce conference in San Francisco was drawing around 180,000 people—the biggest single event in the city every year, selling out hotels within a fifty-mile radius. (For Dreamforce 2015, Salesforce docked a cruise ship at San Francisco so attendees would have rooms to stay in. Talk about chutzpah.) Nobody with a brain buys CRM software anymore, and cloud-based corporate applications have become an accepted part of business. Benioff turned nonconsensus into consensus. Salesforce.com stands as one of the great category kings of the modern era. Marc and Lynne Benioff have donated more than $200 million to children's charities and the Salesforce.com Foundation has a $20 million annual charity budget. Whatever ultimately happens to the company, Marc Benioff will get his plaque in the Category Design Hall of Fame.

The Courage of Category Design

Category design is not for wimps. By definition, category design means stepping out into unknown territory. It requires absolute belief in a category that others can't yet see. You are creating the future you want, not one anyone else has described. You will run into disbelief from customers, analysts, the press, and your own employees. Competitors will mock you. And yet you have to have the courage to push through. As Venrock's Bryan Roberts told us: "Part of being a category king is having the courage to be nonconsensus. Category kings have no model. If you're using a model you've seen elsewhere, you are de facto following."[13]

Elon Musk over and over again has displayed some of the most remarkable courage in category, company, and product building. He envisioned a category of private space companies when it didn't seem like there was even a glimmer of possibility that a private company could solve the problem of making reusable rockets to carry stuff into space. But now SpaceX reigns as the category king of an immensely important new category. In parallel, Musk stuck by his vision for a category of hot electric cars that put gas-powered cars to shame—again, a business that seemed outrageous at the time. And now we have Musk's Tesla Motors. It can be difficult to believe in hindsight, but in early stages Musk was seen as a joke—a dreamer with zero chance of success. Just hanging in there took a ton of will.

We'd like to highlight one seminal act by Musk that demon-strates what kind of courage it can take to design and build a new category. That's when, in 2014, Musk gave away Tesla's patents—a lesson both in courage and in how to think about intellectual property while building a category.

Patents are considered sacred in business, particularly in the technology and pharmaceutical industries. They are sought after as a form of protection—both a wall that can keep enemies at bay, and a weapon that can be wielded to attack competitors. Patents can also be a profit center, generating licensing fees from other com-panies. For all those reasons, patents expressly benefit the company that owns them and hobble potential competitors and other entities entering the same category. That may be fine in a situation like VMware's. Its category caught fire quickly, carrying VMware along with it, and VMware's patents held back powerful players such as Microsoft from building competing products—at least for long enough so that VMware could get established as the clear, undis-puted king. But Tesla faced a different kind of problem in the 2010s. It created a new category and won its crown, but the category was growing slowly. Electric cars are not like a piece of software that can be instantly distributed to the world through the cloud. Cars are expensive and time-consuming to build and distribute. One small company just didn't have the firepower to make the category ex-plode. In 2014 electric cars were still about 1 percent of the total car market. Tesla needed help. It needed to be the king of a thriving category that included competitors, which would help drive up the number of electric cars on the roads, which in turn would help en-courage an ecosystem of charging stations, repair shops, and all the other pieces necessary to develop a burgeoning electric car market. Musk understood that he needed the category to grow so it would demand more of Tesla's cars, even if this meant aiding competitors. As long as Tesla was the category king, the bulk of the benefits of a growing category would accrue to Tesla.

So Musk decided to give away Tesla's patents. He wrote a blog post explaining his decision. The patents, Musk wrote, only served "to stifle progress." By opening up its patents for others to use, Tesla hoped to make it easier for other companies to make great electric cars. "We believe that Tesla, other companies making electric cars, and the world would all benefit from a common, rapidly-evolving technology platform," Musk wrote. To put an exclamation point on his decision, Musk ordered that the framed patents hanging on the wall at Tesla headquarters be taken down.[14]

Musk flew directly in the face of conventional wisdom in order to build his category, knowing that a strong category would be the key to his company's long-term success. This is what we mean by courage. It is the CEO's job to have that courage, and to infuse the rest of the organization with courage.

In technology businesses in particular, categories are being created faster than ever. The king gets crowned faster than ever. The category king takes the majority of the economics. If you're not the king, or at least No. 2, you will be lucky to have much of a business at all. This is about a whole organization leaning forward on its skis when it's already going 80 miles per hour down a double-black-diamond slope. A company has to fully embrace its drive to be a category king, because every part of the organization has to be involved, and every part has to move in synch at maximum speed.

For that reason, the CEO or equivalent leader has to be the driver of category design. It's not a job for the chief marketing officer or the head of product design or any other department head. The leader has to feel the conviction of belief in the category, and bring everyone else along, or else the effort will fail. Companies, we believe, will come to employ category designers, just as they now employ experience and product designers. A category designer can architect a plan for the category and the company, but even then, the CEO will have to drive it because the plan will stretch across so many in-house boundaries. We have worked with a few companies where the CEO or equivalent leader did not completely buy into category king thinking,[15] and that inevitably led to the effort falling short.

We recognize that it's not always easy for entrepreneurs to think this way. Aiming to create a new category where none exists can seem very risky, since by definition there is no market there yet. You have to see something no one can yet see, and if you can't make potential investors, employees, or customers see it, too, they won't want anything to do with your company. The temptation instead is to pick out a well-trodden category and go after a crumb of it. By doing that you have a shot at a minor success. You might carve out a little corner of a category with a me-too product that has a new feature or a slight twist, and in the end sell your company to Google or Facebook for what to most of the working universe would seem like a winning lottery ticket. You walk away with a million dollars, your company disappears into the maw of some giant, and no one really remembers what you'd done. If that's you, you should grab a beer from the fridge and maybe go out and buy a Mustang and enjoy life. We can respect that. But you might as well put this book down, because you're not our audience.

Then again, if you believe that the best strategy is to do everything you can to increase your odds of becoming a category king and an enduring company . . . our playbook follows.

Part II

The Category King Playbook

(Or, the Part About
How Pirates, Dreamers, and
Innovators Create and Dominate
Markets)

4

Start: How to Discover a Category

Inspiration to Insight

We said early in the book that failure is a feature, not a bug. You learn a lot from failure.[1] Early in his career, Paul Martino took part in one of the most costly breakdowns of category discovery and design we can think of—costly in terms of lost future potential. Martino in 2003 cofounded Tribe Networks with Mark Pincus (who later founded Zynga) and Valerie Syme. Tribe was one of the early social networks, founded about the same time as MySpace and a year before Facebook. Tribe's initial insight that the Internet was creating a new way for people to socialize was directionally right, of course. But Tribe struggled to find a way to define and develop the space. It kept revamping its product and experience depending on what users were demanding—in other words, letting customers design the category, which is rarely a good idea. Tribe couldn't get much traction in the market, and of course Facebook eventually defined and took control of the social networking category and became one of the great category kings of all time. Tribe faded to black. "Those were some of the most painful days of my entrepreneurial career," Martino says now.[2] As of this writing, Facebook was worth $233 billion, about the same as Wal-Mart.

So anyway, Martino went on to start a couple of other companies and then, in 2010, founded investment firm Bullpen Capital.

The firm found a niche in Silicon Valley, investing in companies in between the very earliest seed rounds that companies get when starting out, yet before the first venture capital players come in with a lot more money at Series A. The Bullpen name is a baseball metaphor for its strategy: "Kind of like the middle relief pitcher who comes in to bridge the gap between the starting pitcher and the closer," Martino says. And Bullpen has been quite successful in this game, thanks in part to Martino's category lessons learned from Tribe. He looks for companies that have a crazy, nonconsensus, one-of-a-kind idea, but he also has to see that the company has the mindset to turn that idea into a category.

As part of the process for finding those companies, on every third Friday of the month Bullpen hosts a session it calls the Fullpen. About a dozen people—Bullpen partners and invited guests—park around a conference room table. Over the course of a couple of hours, two or three entrepreneurs come in and pitch their company ideas. Some will walk away with nothing except advice. A few will get a Bullpen investment.

Dave (one of your authors) is a regular at Fullpen sessions, where he's come to be known as the category guy. He asks three questions of these entrepreneurs, who are usually young and quite nervous. These are becoming known as Dave's Three Questions:[3]

1. Can you explain to me like a five-year-old what problem you're trying to solve?
2. If your company solves this problem perfectly, what category are you in?
3. If you win 85 percent of that category, what's the size of your category potential?

A lot of the entrepreneurs come into a Fullpen session with an initial insight or idea that by itself seems pretty interesting. Maybe it's a service that doesn't yet exist, or a technology advance that does something that couldn't be done before. But rare is the entrepreneur who can answer Dave's Three Questions. That's when the trapdoor in the Fullpen room floor opens and the entrepreneur disappears into a crocodile pit.[4]

The questions get at what the Fullpen participants need to know—in fact, what the world needs to know—about the entrepreneurs' insights. Is what you're creating just a cool thing and little more? Is it a feature of someone else's category? Or can it blossom into its own vital, dynamic category? An insight by itself isn't worth much. An insight has to lead to discovering a category that fits with the company and product you can build.

Still, an insight is where you have to start. So how do you get one?

Most of the best insights come from what we call a "missing." Basically, someone sees something that they feel is missing from the world, and the person is driven to fill that void. Google's Larry Page felt he had to harness hyperlinks to fix search. Mark Zuckerberg had to create an online version of the Harvard freshman "facebook" so he could more easily meet girls. Clarence Birdseye had to bring frozen food to the masses, inspired by what he saw in the arctic. Jack O'Neill always said he had to invent the surfing wetsuit because he wanted to find a way to surf longer in cold water. Les Paul had to create the electric guitar so he could be heard. "I used to play the harmonica and guitar," Paul once told an interviewer, "and one time I was playing in the parking lot of a barbecue joint, and a guy told me, 'Your harmonica is fine, but your guitar isn't loud enough.' That got to me, so I got to thinking about how to make a louder guitar."[5]

Some of the best thinking about insights that we've encountered come from another early-stage investment firm, Floodgate, and its principals Ann Miura-Ko and Mike Maples.[6] They look for one of two types of insights: *market insights* and *technology insights*. Here's how that works:

MARKET INSIGHTS:

A market insight involves seeing a "missing" in the world at large and believing that technology can be built to solve it. Les Paul had a market insight. He realized there was a need for an amplified guitar, believed that technology could be applied to fix that situation, and was overwhelmed by the feeling that he had to be the one to do it. He saw the need first, then built the technology to meet the need. Similarly, the Uber guys had a market insight, seeing the "missing" in taxicab hailing and believing technology could fix it.

How do you get one of these market insights? Many of the great ones come from an intersection of a person's knowledge and passion swizzled with serendipity. The serendipity is like the guy in the parking lot telling Les Paul he couldn't hear his guitar. That knowledge/serendipity combination is behind the story of Evan Spiegel and Snapchat. Spiegel grew up as a privileged kid in Southern California, the eldest child of two high-powered lawyers. By the time he attended Stanford, Spiegel was the kind of wealthy, connected, snowboarding, BMW-driving party guy who would've been at home in an episode of *Entourage*. Such a guy apparently had quite a bit of experience with women sending him potentially embarrassing photos, which got him thinking about a missing: Spiegel believed there would be a market for a way to send images or text that would automatically disappear. He was at Stanford, steeping in the school's computer science and start-up milieu, providing him with knowledge of the possibilities of new technology. So he pursued his disappearing-picture idea, originally called Picaboo. Picaboo soon became Snapchat, and Spiegel's market insight evolved into a full-blown media property and turned into a business valued at billions of dollars.[7]

Flipkart is an example of a market insight that grew out of an intersection of culture, geography, and technology. In 2007, Amazon was well established around the globe but ran into headwinds in India. Regulations there prevented Amazon from selling directly to consumers from its own inventory, so shipping from afar might cost $9 on a $10 book. The postal service was unreliable and a vast swath of potential customers either didn't have a credit card or shied from using credit cards online. Sachin Bansal and Binny Bansal had both graduated from the prestigious technology university IIT-Delhi and actually went to work for Amazon in India, so they understood Amazon's problems there firsthand— yet also saw a yawning opportunity. Their market insight: India needed a uniquely Indian online retailer. So the two set up Flipkart, and built their own warehouses and a delivery system suited to the culture. Thousands of Flipkart's couriers would put products into their backpacks and ride off on motorbikes to pick their way through the perpetually jammed streets of India's cities. At a customer's door, they'd take cash for the purchase, bypassing credit cards entirely. The service caught on among Indian consumers, and in mid-2015 Flipkart raised funding at a $15 billion valuation. "A simple desire to create a tailor made product for the Indian consumer has grown into something beyond what we imagined," Sachin Bansal told the *Hindu*.[8]

Marc Benioff and Jeff Bezos more methodically pursued their market insights. Benioff, as we showed earlier, already worked deep inside the software industry, at Oracle. He knew all about CRM software, and to him CRM's shortcomings were the "missing" in that industry. He saw the nascent Internet as the technology he could apply to fix it. Bezos also realized the Internet would be a game changer, though at first he wasn't sure what game it would change. While working on Wall Street in 1994, "I came across a fact that Web usage was growing at 2,300 percent a year," he told us. "I had never seen anything growing 2,300 percent a year, so the question for me was: what kind of business plan might make sense in the context of this growth?" He made a list of twenty products that could effectively be sold through mail order, and studied each. Books were on that list, and Bezos concluded books had an interesting trait: no bookstore could carry more than 100,000 or so titles, but millions of books were in print. He could use the Internet to launch the world's largest bookstore. When Amazon.com went live in 1995, it offered a million titles in its catalog. Bezos had worked his way through logic to arrive at a market insight.[9]

Of course, all these market insights look obvious in retrospect. But at the time, they were not. It was not obvious there was a market for an electric guitar, DVDs by mail, surf wetsuits, or books over the Internet. It was also not obvious that these entrepreneurs could build the technology, companies, and categories that would make the insights come alive. And that's the other trick about market insights. When you have a good one, it seems a little crazy. It is nonconsensus. It becomes your job to make it consensus, and to believe in it when no one else does.

TECHNOLOGY INSIGHTS:

A technology insight usually comes from a scientist or engineer. The "missing" is entirely about the technology itself. An inventor sees a way to create something that's never before existed, often hoping that a worthwhile problem can be found that the invention will solve. "Technology doesn't always translate into product power," Miura-Ko tells us. "Technology can be in search of a problem."[10] The VMware founders had a technology insight. They saw how to virtualize computers before understanding what problem virtualization solved. Birdseye started with a technology insight—a way to flash-freeze fish. Inventions ranging from Bell's telephone and the Wright brothers' airplane to buckyballs and human genome sequencing started as technology insights that had not yet translated into product power.

Skype resulted from what might be one of the more bizarre technology insights ever. The story started in 1999, when Niklas Zennstrom, from Sweden, and Janus Friis, from Denmark, left their jobs at a Swedish telecommunications company to start what was essentially a criminal operation: the file-sharing site Kazaa. You might remember that Kazaa was part of the early wave, along with Napster, of sites accused of stealing recorded music. While Zennstrom and Friis worked out of Amsterdam, Kazaa was largely built by contracted programmers in Estonia. By 2001 various government and music industry entities worked to shut down Kazaa and sue Zennstrom and Friis. To protect themselves, Zennstrom and Friis shuffled Kazaa off to other ownership based in Vanuatu, an island nation near Australia known for a popular cultural activity called land diving, which pretty much involves diving off towers over dry land. (Yup!) The duo then realized that the technology behind Kazaa could be used in other ways. They brainstormed and figured the technology could solve the problem of expensive international phone calls—by making those calls free over the Net. The Estonians again got tapped to write the code. In 2003, Zennstrom and Friis founded Skype and released it on the Internet. By 2010, Skype had about 660 million worldwide users.[11] Two pirates found a way to lower the cost and increase the access of global communication in a way that has made a difference to millions. In 2011, Microsoft purchased Skype for $8.5 billion.

Pixar started its life with a technology insight that never converted into a significant category, but over time the company used that technology insight to find the right category. Ed Catmull was a computer scientist who grew up loving Disney animation. He believed computers could be made to create animation—a technology insight he chased from the time he entered the University of Utah. But he at first thought his category was animation-making computers—and his company's first product was the Pixar Image Computer. The plan was to sell these machines to moviemakers. In 1986, Steve Jobs bought Pixar, thinking he was buying a computer company. It proved to be a terrible business. Only about three hundred Pixar Image Computers were ever sold, and the company plunged into the red. But when Pixar's future looked bleak, Catmull's creative collaborator, John Lasseter, who previously helped Pixar make a short demo film, proposed that Pixar use its own technology to make its own movie. That movie, the first full-length computer-animated feature, was *Toy Story*. It debuted in 1995 and set Pixar on a course to become one of the most influential movie companies in history. Pixar found a way to turn its technology insight into product power and create a massive new category in the film industry.[12]

In the end, a market or technology insight only matters if it leads to good answers to Dave's Three Questions. *Can you explain what problem you're trying to solve?* To create a category, that problem needs to be one that people didn't realize they had or didn't realize they could solve. *If your company solves this problem perfectly, what category are you in?* It needs to be a category that doesn't exist and that you have the ability to create. It must be nonconsensus or you are by default a follower. *If you win 85 percent of that category, what's the size of your category potential?* The answer tells the world how big your company can become and how much your company will matter. Are you Pixar in its first phase, with a category potential of three hundred machines? Or are you Pixar in its second phase, with category potential of dominating a global computer-animated movie category that never before existed but is now worth hundreds of billions of dollars over the course of decades?

Insight to Category

Entrepreneurs can be great at coming up with a market or technology insight, but too few take the next step and discover the category that fits that insight. They seem to have an unquestioned belief that once the world sees their new product, the world will "get it," and so these innovators leave the category to chance. History teaches us the entrepreneurs who are also category designers better their odds of success by being systematic about category discovery.

We'll share with you how we do our work to help a company arrive at a category, though we're not saying it's the *only* way to do this work. We're saying it's important to go through a process like this, do the research internally and externally, and think the way a category king might think. We at Play Bigger are not the magicians who come up with a "missing" and connect it to a category—we take entrepreneurs and executives through a process that helps *them* do that. The goal is for them to condition the market to see the missing the way the entrepreneur does. If the world embraces the problem, it will literally demand the solution from the category king.

To give you a view into this process, we'd like to introduce you to Origami Logic and its CEO, Opher Kahane. He cofounded the company with Ofer Shaked and Alon Amit in 2012. Kahane and Shaked had gone to school together in Israel and all three cofounders served in Israel's equivalent of the U.S. National Security Agency, getting an intense education in the kinds of things these organizations do: massive data collection, analytics, and intelligence. After his military service, Kahane played a role in building VocalTec, an Israeli company that was one of the first to put voice calls over the Internet,[13] then he moved to the United States and started another voice-over-Internet company called Kagoor Networks, which got bought by Juniper Networks in 2005. Meanwhile, Shaked founded Yahoo Answers, and Amit got a Ph.D. in math and joined Google and, later, Facebook. By the time they got together and formed Origami, these guys were anything but rookies. And in fact if you look back at media stories about Origami's first funding rounds in 2012, you get the sense that investors were investing because of the team, not so much because Origami could clearly answer Dave's Three Questions. When *Tech-Crunch* wrote about Accel Partners leading a Series A round of $9.3

million for Origami, the story said: "According to partner Jake Flomenberg, part of the attraction here for Accel and the others is the fact that Kahane and his co founders . . . have collectively years of experience as successful entrepreneurs."[14] In other words, Accel was saying: "We bet on the team, not the idea."

Origami from the start said it was a marketing intelligence company. Now, "marketing intelligence" is a vast and chaotic landscape of many different kinds of companies. It's certainly not a category, and it doesn't have a king. Origami saying it's in marketing intelligence is like a writer who specializes in historical novels about eighteenth-century British royalty saying she's in the business of "writing." In its little corner of the marketing tech bedlam, Origami built marketing technology that's based on the kind of massive data scouring the founders learned from Israeli intelligence. Origami's system collects and analyzes every kind of marketing blip and ping from all over the Internet, including transactions, page views, tweets, video plays, conversations on social networks, and mentions in media or anywhere else a product might be discussed. Kahane described Origami as a "control tower for marketers." He would add: "The platform sucks in all the data [marketers] care about and makes it accessible in a way that's useful and valuable for them." The system is complex, involving data warehousing, analytics, business intelligence visualization, and a user interface that Kahane describes as "the equivalent of a Facebook feed for what's going on in your marketing data."[15]

Kahane's language didn't much help distinguish Origami or define its unique power to solve a unique problem. The company started in 2012 with a technology insight—these guys knew how to take their data science experience and build technology that could do stuff with marketing data no one could do before. But by 2015, they needed to connect the technology insight to a category they could own. Otherwise, they risked getting lost among the zillion marketing-tech products and services swirling around potential customers. Kahane was in search of a way to "identify and define the rules of engagement, which starts with defining the problem and defining a way to solve it."

The process of category design starts with discovery—looking for those critical insights with the team through a series of conversations, interviews, whiteboarding sessions, or drinks. That insight is always there, but sometimes it is buried under heaps of day-to-day minutiae and can take weeks to unearth. Sometimes it is sitting on the surface. The trick is to spot it, listen for it, and push it around to make sure you really know it when you see it. This becomes the first phase of real category design, converting insight into a plan for a worthy category, a compelling story, and a course of action for conditioning the market to see the world the way you do.

Let's start with the category discovery work with Origami.

Our job was to help the company's brilliant technologists and entrepreneurs understand what they already knew. At Origami, we started by interviewing a select set of executives, board members, leaders, and external advisors. Each interview typically took forty-five minutes to an hour. We'd ask them a series of targeted questions to get them to talk about eleven different facets of the company. Those facets:

Vision mission: What was the original market or technology insight that led you to create this company?

Customers: Who do you envision buying this product or service? Who will use it?

Problem statement: What's the problem you think you can solve for your potential customers?

Use cases: What are the specific ways people will use this product or service to solve their problem?

Product/solution: Give a detailed explanation of the technology behind the solution—what does it do now, and what else is it capable of doing?

Ecosystem: In many cases there are other companies involved in solving the problem or adding additional value. These companies form an ecosystem around the problem and solution. What are all the companies and where in the ecosystem are the control points where one company has leverage?

Competition: Who else is trying to solve this problem—or, if no one else sees the problem yet, who might jump in to compete with you to solve the problem once you identify it?

Business model: How will your product or service change business for your customers? Will it increase their return on investment or reduce costs in a significant way? Or does it allow them to do something that couldn't have been done with prior technology, creating huge value?

Sales and go-to-market: Enterprise companies should articulate how the product or solution will make its way to the market. Through a sales force? Through distribution partners? Both? For a consumer company, how will users find out about your solution? From app stores? Search? Viral adoption? Growth hacking techniques? Advertising? PR?

Organization: How is the company organized? Who are the major influencers on the company? How are decisions made? What kind of culture will work?

Funding strategy: What's the next funding event? A private financing? An IPO? How much runway does the company have before it needs more money and what kind of funding is in place to execute against the category strategy?

Those are the types of questions we ask insiders. But it's also important to look outside—at the space around the company. For Origami, that meant surveying the entire marketing-tech landscape. What categories exist already? Who sucks in the space and who is good? Is anybody good? Who are the thought leaders—analysts, bloggers, press, investors? What do they say? We found that the marketing-tech landscape around Origami was a chaotic mess. There is no way any company should want to say its category is marketing technology. It's not even a category. It's a stampede of drunks to an open bar.

Origami needed to design a category centered on its technology insight, and the category had to fit snugly with the culture and capabilities of the company going forward. The category needed to set Origami off on its own, beside or above the stampede. Most of all, the category needed to clearly be tied to the problem it was solving, which had to be a problem that potential customers didn't yet know they had, or didn't know could be solved. The way to discover that problem and category was to force the company to think about itself and its space in a deep, detailed way. It's sort of like putting the company on a psychologist's couch and making the patient confront the details of his or her life. This, we find, is fundamentally different from the usual practice of rushing to build and release the product, believing a great product will speak for itself.

As Origami went through this process, it started to see how its technology insight connected to a unique problem. The company had to understand the from/to it would need to create. The first step involved identifying the customer—who inside companies actually cares about this marketing-tech shit? Usually it's the head of analytics, the person who runs digital marketing, and the chief marketing officer. Where were each of those types of customers coming from, and where did Origami want to move them to? Put another way, what's the problem they don't know they have or don't know they can solve, and what would their world look like if they had a solution? Most of the time, the from/to—or froto—discussion gets lively, and in the end it generates an understanding of the customer and a collective vision for the future.

The froto discussion at Origami led to a first sketch of the category. Origami saw that its technology was a way to move

marketing measurement from an art to a science; from interpreta-
tion to fact; from lagging spreadsheet reports to real-time reporting. It could solve the problem of taking something blurred and
mushy and making it sharp and tangible. The conversation then
turned to how to use such attributes to define a category.

Naming a category is part art, part science. Lots of companies
have hired a branding agency to help pick a three-letter acronym
that describes their product or service, but naming a category has
to involve more rigorous thinking. It's not like naming your cat:
"Do I like this name or not?" The right thinking leads to a name
that will help design and dominate a new large space. The name
will inform the strategy of the company, not the other way around.
A category name should describe the nature of the problem being
solved. For companies aimed at the enterprise, the name should
speak to the business function where the problem lives. Ideally,
the category name will become a line item in every company's
budget. Consumer-facing companies need a category name that's
direct and descriptive, like "social network" or "on-demand transportation." The art of naming a category comes into play when
choosing the right words to convey all the right attributes.

At Origami, the team wrestled with conflicting directions for
the name. On one hand, they felt a desire to make the category
very functional. Another urge was to make the category famil-
iar sounding, setting it close to existing analytics and intelligence
technology, so customers would feel a sense of comfort that Origami wasn't some overreaching solution that was more science
fiction than science. Yet one way or another, the category had to
break free of the mar-tech noise and establish high ground with a
new discipline in marketing.

So we helped Origami develop a category name that tried to hit
the intersection of the Wild West of exploding marketing platforms and the needs of a marketing executive who has to run campaigns across an increasingly complex product and organizational

matrix. Our first shot at a name: Marketing Channel Measurement and Analytics.

And . . . to Origami's credit, they hated it. They hated the words *channel* and *analytics* and wanted to be more visionary. Things got heated, emotional—which is all good. A passionate dialogue is how good things ultimately happen. The Origami team tabled the discussion for a couple of days to let the ideas sink in. It turned into a week of discussion before a much better name surfaced: Origami named the new category Marketing Signal Measurement. The category name is meant to crystallize a new "thing" called marketing signals, culled from every corner of the digital landscape. And if marketers want to measure marketing signals, who are they going to call? Probably the company that identified marketing signals and how to measure them in the first place—and that would be Origami.

Discovering and describing the category is only a beginning. A CEO or leader needs to go on a mission to enroll the world in his or her ideas. Evangelism matters. It's up to Kahane and his team to make the category real and enduring, and to make sure Origami is the king. (As of this writing, that's yet to play out.) As we've been saying, a category king designs a product, company, and category at the same time. Kahane wonderfully stated what he sees as his challenge and responsibility: "The category name is not going to work on its own out of the box," he told us. "We needed to pick a name and we have to *make* it work."

Once a company discovers its category, it must fully embrace the category internally. The category has to become part of the very fabric of the company. The CEO at this stage transforms into the chief category officer, taking on the task of convincing management and employees to buy in. Workshops, dinners, or any kind of session that stirs discussion about the category and how to design it becomes critical. Everyone needs to start thinking that their jobs are to design a category, company, and product that fit together and amplify each other. This is also the time to keep an eye out for what we call a Zed[16]—the person (and there always is one!) who doesn't believe in the category and will work to sabotage it. A persuasive Zed on the executive team will waste time and sap energy from the category design process. If you spot a Zed inside your company as it goes through category design, eject that person from the company immediately. Send a strong message to other potential Zeds that if they don't get with the program, they'll get sent home.

As the company internalizes and debates the category, it should sketch out what the category means to every part of the company. What does it mean for the product and its features? What does it mean for marketing and sales, for the types of investors you'll pitch, for the partners you might approach? This is where the shit gets real and any resistance to the category decision will come flying out of the cupboards like a cat in a horror film. We will discuss more about this phase in future chapters.

This much has to be clear: Once you know your category, it becomes your true north. It must guide all of your journeys.

Insight to Category: A Story That's Not Origami

We told Origami's story because we wanted you to see the process from inside a well-funded Silicon Valley start-up. We've also studied a cross section of category kings, looking at how they moved from original insight to discovering a category. Category kings always go through some form of this passage from insight to category, but it's rarely planned or methodical. The companies that pull it off are pretty lucky—some had a leader who instinctively drove the discovery, some had it happen by accident, in some cases it arose out of the stress of a crisis or near-death experience. But the point is that *they were lucky*. You can rely on luck—or you can take it upon yourself to methodically do the work to move from insight to category, and increase your odds.

For a glimpse at what the process looks like when it's messier, we had a chance to ask Airbnb CEO Brian Chesky about that company's passage from insight to category discovery. Airbnb started with a market insight so inconsequential, it's a miracle the company ever got any bigger. In 2007, Chesky and his roommate, Joe Gebbia, lived in San Francisco and could barely afford their rent. When a major conference rolled into town and attendees soaked up all the local hotel rooms at jacked-up prices, Chesky and Gebbia bought three air mattresses and posted a notice on the Internet offering a bed for the night and breakfast in the morning. Air mattresses plus bed plus breakfast equaled Airbedandbreakfast. Their market insight: they could sell extra space in people's homes during major events in different cities. Chesky and Gebbia brought in a third partner, Nathan Blecharczyk, and in 2008 they launched Airbedandbreakfast.com. The name eventually got shortened to Airbnb.com.

"For a while we kind of wondered as we started building Airbnb what sort of business we were in," Chesky told us. "We thought we were kind of a marketplace for space."[17] The company started expanding beyond selling air beds during big events and created a website where people could find places to crash in any city at any time. The whole enterprise had a laid-back, sharing-economy, Millennial-generation feel to it, and a small out-of-the-mainstream accidental category took shape around online couch surfing. For a few years Airbnb mostly just went with the flow, taking each next logical step without really seeing the destination. If people wanted to use Airbnb to rent space on couches, maybe they'd want to rent a whole extra bedroom. Boom—it worked. How about renting a whole apartment or house? Boom—worked again. Hosts grew from college kids seeking extra beer money to absentee landlords renting out multiple properties. Around 2013, amid willy-nilly growth, Chesky realized he didn't have control of his category. He didn't have a strong story. And so everyone in Airbnb's ecosystem—employees, investors, hosts, customers, analysts, media—had different ideas of what Airbnb was all about and where it was going. "I remember [over] Christmas, I was learning about hospitality," Chesky said. "And then it dawned on us, 'My God! We're a hospitality company!' And if you look up hospitality, you talk about hospitality, it means welcoming somebody as if they're in your home."

But no way could Airbnb just say it's in the "hospitality" business. First of all, it's not really a category, for the same reason Origami wouldn't want to be a "marketing tech" company, Airbnb would get lost as a hospitality company and it would risk running headlong into the hotel industry. If the public thought Airbnb was solving the same problem as hotels—a room to stay in while traveling—then Airbnb would always seem like a subchoice behind the established hotel industry.

So Chesky kept thinking about it. "Hospitality is what hotels do, and we at Airbnb are totally different than that," he said. "What we do that's different than hotels is we deliver hospitality through community, and so we're a community-driven hospitality company, and that was the kind of revelation we had. When that happened, it completely changed a lot of the ways we thought about things." Now, "community-driven hospitality" may not be the most well-named category on the planet, but still—having a sense of category, of purpose, of destiny made an enormous difference at Airbnb. It focused the company's ecosystem and gave it a distinct direction. It helped the public see Airbnb as solving a unique problem: where to stay when you want a different, more eclectic, more socially networked alternative to cookie-cutter hotels. The company caught fire. By 2015 it had more rooms available than any hotel company, and was valued at $24 billion.[18] Airbnb so powerfully owned the category that the name Airbnb became a synonym for the whole category.

Airbnb's journey from insight to category to expression was closer to the experience of most category kings. The company didn't go through a disciplined process. But at least Chesky under-stood that the company had to go through some version of coming to deeply understand the company and its space. Airbnb had to discover and articulate its rightful place in the universe. Every category king has to do this, and there are infinite ways to carry it out. Our version is the result of us learning from what has worked in our careers and what's worked for companies we've studied. We are trying to help entrepreneurs, inventors, and executives turn an undisciplined, accidental search for a category into a disciplined process that anyone can adopt.

Discovering the category is hard to get right, and costly to get wrong. But everything else flows from that discovery. Nothing else works until you can answer Dave's Three Questions. Once you have those down, you can get to work building the product, company, and category that will ignite market pull.

The Play Bigger Guide to Category Discovery and Expression

Step One: Start with "Who"

The first question: Who is going to lead the work to discover and name the category? Certainly the founders or CEO must be completely committed to the work, but in most cases they aren't the right choices for actually doing the work. Just as it's tough to psychoanalyze yourself, it's tough for a founding team to back away and look at the company with fresh eyes, avoiding tangles of politics, product features, and emotions. There's a reason Mac-romedia's CEO asked Al, Dave, and Christopher to come in from outside to assess the company's "bag of doorknobs" and create a category. We're not trying to convince you to hire our firm—as we said in the Introduction, we're not telling you this so we can build an intergalactic mega-consultancy death star. (That would be our nightmare!) We're saying you probably need to hand this work to someone (or a small group) who can come in fresh, whether that's an outsider, a new board member, a newly hired executive, or a category design firm.

At a large, successful existing company most executives get paid to *not* fuck things up. They don't get paid to identify green-field category potential and go for it.[19] At a start-up, the founding team is often madly working eighty hours a week to keep the company on track—they don't have the time or excess brain capacity to take on this work. And this work takes time—not just to go through the process, but to think.

So, step one: Figure out who.

Step Two: Fact Finding

Once you choose someone to do the work, have that person interview every senior leader in the company, plus key board members and external advisors. Outside research is important, too. Pull together analyst reports, search the Web, see how the media covers the space. One thing to kick to the curb is customer focus groups. When designing new categories, customer opinions can actually be deadly. New categories are nonconsensus. Customers don't yet know they want them. If Manoj Bhargava had asked customers if they wanted an energy shot, they would have likely said no—or "What the hell is an energy shot?"

The questions to explore, as stated earlier in the chapter:

Vision mission: What was the original market or technology insight that led you to create this company?

Customers: Who do you envision buying this product or service? Who will use it?

Problem statement: What's the problem you think you can solve for your potential customers?

Use cases: What are the specific ways people will use this product or service to solve their problem?

Product/solution: Give a detailed explanation of the technology behind the solution—what does it do now, and what else is it capable of doing?

Ecosystem: In many cases there are other companies involved in solving the problem or adding additional value. These companies form an ecosystem around the problem and solution. What are all the companies and where in the ecosystem are the control points where one company has leverage?

Competition: Who else is trying to solve this problem—or, if no one else sees the problem yet, who might jump in to compete with you to solve the problem once you identify it?

Business model: How will your product or service change business for your customers? Will it increase their return on investment or reduce costs in a significant way? Or does it allow them to do something that couldn't have been done with prior technology, creating huge value?

Sales and go-to-market: Enterprise companies should articulate how the product or solution will make its way to the market. Through a sales force? Through distribution partners? For a consumer company, how will users find out about your solution? From app stores? Search? Growth hacking techniques? Advertising?

Organization: How is the company organized? Who are the major influencers on the company? How are decisions made?

Funding strategy: What's the next funding event? A private financing? An IPO? How much runway does the company have before it needs more money and what kind of funding is in place to execute against the category strategy?

When the interviews and research are complete, the interviewer or interview team should gather notes and facts and think through provocative ways to stimulate discussion of categories and category names.

Step Three: Workshop

Next step is a workshop with the CEO and leadership team. The category king workshop is half educational and half engaged discussion and debate. We recommend taking a full day to unplug and focus on this discussion.

The educational part is setting the context. It should be a presentation to the assembled group. Everyone needs to understand why category is the new strategy and why it's imperative in the current era to become a category king. They also need to understand the landscape around the company as it currently exists, before the company changes it by identifying a new problem to be solved.

The rest of the time, stir up a lively debate. The topics should be tackled in order:

WHO ARE THE CUSTOMERS?

Identify the kinds of people you're addressing now and the kinds of people you really want to address. Talk about who they are, what they do, and why they might want your shit.

WHAT'S THE PROBLEM THEY DON'T YET KNOW THEY HAVE OR CAN'T YET SOLVE?

This starts requiring some imagination. Presumably, if you've come this far, you're convinced you have some kind of market or technology insight—so you see something potential customers don't yet see. How do you frame your insight from the customer's point of view? What would make them have the same aha you had?

WHAT ARE THE FROM/TOS?

Once you identify the problem, what's the solution? What's the journey customers need to take to reject an old way of doing things and embrace your new way of doing things?

WHAT'S THE NEW "THING"?

If those are the from/tos, then what would be the new thing that every person or company has to have to make that journey? Origami identified "marketing signals." Airbnb identified "community-driven hospitality." Les Paul identified "electric guitar." What's your new thing that never existed before but that your customers will feel they must have?

One big benefit of this workshop is to (a) focus the leadership team on the core issues of category design and (b) make sure each member of the leadership team hears what everyone else is saying about each of these topics. Too often one dominant voice drowns out everyone else. The purpose of the workshop is to make sure everyone is heard and involved.

Step Four: Name That Category

Do all of the aforementioned work and the category will start to emerge. Talk about words that would describe the category, and what kind of impact those words would have on the customers you want to influence. Keep in mind that the words will become a north star for the company, influencing strategy and execution across all departments. Keep it simple, powerful, clear, and different. The words shouldn't describe your specific product—they should describe the category of product you make. Yet the product you make should be the unique solution to the problem the category identifies.

Play with combinations of two or three words—hardly ever

more than that. The team might have an epiphany and land on a category name everyone instantly loves. But that's not how it usually goes down. As happened at Origami, you might land on a name that doesn't quite sit right. Stop there, table it for a few days, and then come back to the discussion. And even then, remember what Origami's Kahane said: the name might not ever be perfect, but it becomes the company's job to grab hold of the category name it chooses and *make* it perfect—make it seem like it was inevitable all along.

Step Five: Package the Work

We package the discussions and information gained during the workshop into a category design document. The document addresses the following topics:

Category Landscape—what the category you create would look like and where it fits.

Category Ecosystem—the customers, competitors, developers, suppliers, analysts, media, and everyone else who would plug into the category.

Frotos—the from/to journey you want customers to take.

Category Name and Description—the final version.

The Case for the New Category—write out why the category should exist and what the world will look like if the company creates and dominates the category.

Early Draft Game Plan—a sketch of how the company can create and dominate the category.

We usually need ten revisions of these documents before we are ready to share them. We intentionally do not involve the executive team in the first round of developing these decks. We then reveal them at a meeting of the senior team. The reactions are usually visceral and Dave, who is an expert in reading body language from all his years as a poker player, is on high alert reading signs from the team. We all take a ton of notes to capture the responses, and we keep an eye out for the Zed—the person who seems intent on derailing the whole process. The purpose of packaging and presenting a category design document is to refine it, nail it down, and get complete buy-in. Once you commit to the new category, there is no turning back. You've got to burn the boats.

During this phase we will often find ourselves in front of the investors or board presenting our findings and recommendations—in support of the CEO, who is leading the charge at this point. More feedback, more reactions, more refinement.

And then we have it: a category discovered, identified, and thoroughly expressed for internal consumption. At the moment, the work begins to craft a point of view—the category's story. This POV will form the guiding principles of the company's strategy—something of a United States Declaration of Independence, declaring the truths that the company holds as self-evident.

For details about the POV, read on . . .

5

Strategy: The Power of a Point of View

A Quick Comparison Study

This is a bad point of view. Unfortunately, it could be the POV of any of a thousand companies in technology.

> Mega-Tech-Ding-Dong Corp., headquartered in San Jose, Calif., is a leading developer and global supplier of innovative high-speed, world-class cloud infrastructure platform application solutions to worldwide global 2000 customers in all industries. Mega-Tech-Ding-Dong's big data application infrastructure platform solutions are highly scalable, reliable, flexible, and powerful. Built by a world-class team that possesses in-depth understanding of applicable global communication standards, software and hardware expertise in design, architecture and development of standard-based, open, social, IoT, mobile, wireless, container-enabled, distributed, hyper-converged computing systems, our technology leverages existing investments to create solutions which deliver high levels of performance, ROI and value to the business.

And now, here's a great POV.

How Stories Make a King

Stories have always been an industrial-strength force in human progress, from the epic poems of Homer to the tales of Marco Polo, Shakespeare's historical plays, the novels of Ayn Rand, and biographies of Steve Jobs. Stories alter perspectives and exert influence. When traders on Wall Street consider a stock, they often ask, "What's the story?" When pitching a venture capitalist, entrepreneurs get funding when they craft a great story, and now a cottage industry offers pitch training. Raw information reaches us on an intellectual level, but stories reach into our hearts and our pants. Stories form deep grooves. Decades of brain research have demonstrated that stories have a more lasting impact than facts. One 1969 Stanford study, "Narrative Stories as Mediators for Serial Learning," showed that students remembered six to seven times more words embedded in a story compared to random words.[1] In the 2010s, Paul Zak, a professor at Claremont Graduate University, found that character-driven attention-grabbing stories actually increase oxytocin in the brain. Oxytocin is an empathy chemical, and it motivates cooperation and understanding—quite important when trying to convince someone to, as Apple used to say, think different. "My experiments show that character-driven stories with emotional content result in a better understanding of the key points a speaker wishes to make and enable better recall of these points weeks later," Zack wrote. He added a swipe at the way too much business has been conducted for far too long: "In terms of making an impact, [storytelling] blows the standard Power-Point presentation to bits."[2]

That's why category designers tell a story. We call that story a point of view, or POV. After you come up with an aha of an initial market or technology insight, and after you discover and define the right category, you have to craft the story about the category that you'll tell. You need a powerful POV.

A POV tells the world you're a company on a mission, not a missionary company looking to make money any way it can. It frames the new problem that your category identifies, and sets you up as the answer. When someone can articulate your problem, you believe that person must have the solution. It's why Bill Clinton won two presidential elections by claiming, "I feel your pain," and why Ronald Reagan beat Jimmy Carter by simply asking, "Are you better off than you were four years ago?" Politicians are masters at this.

A great POV separates the companies, products, and categories that people love from the ones they, at best, tolerate. When you start to think about it, you can easily see the difference between a company that has a strong POV and one that has a POV black hole. In grocery stores, you can sense that Whole Foods has a clear POV, built around healthy gourmet products, while Safeway seems to have no POV at all other than selling groceries. Southwest Airlines has a palpable POV; United Airlines does not. Apple has a POV; Microsoft does not.[3]

A POV conditions the market to accept and embrace the company's vision and have the same aha the founders experienced. The story leads potential customers on their from/to journey, so they understand both what is missing and why your company can fix that problem. A POV has to shift people's minds so they reject an old way of thinking and come to believe in something new. It has to reach people on an emotional level. No one remembers what you say—but they remember how you made them feel. That feeling can be excitement about something that's coming, or fear of missing out. Some of the best POVs make people think: "Oh fuck, I don't have one of those! *I have to get one of those!*" To reach people's emotions, a POV has to sound the way people talk. It has to be simple, direct, visceral. Language matters! Nobody in the history of the human race has ever been moved to joy or tears by a train wreck of lazy business babble. The story about your business is more important than the facts about your business. Sound outrageous? Maybe, but the brain research proves it's true. People relate to and remember stories—even people who make a living analyzing facts.

A POV tells a story with a beginning, middle, and end. It tells the world why this category and the company creating it are *different*. Different sticks. Different forces a choice between what was and what can be. A POV built around *better* is about comparing your offering to the thing customers already know. *Better* reinforces the power of the category king you're trying to beat (who by definition is not you). If customers think two companies are tied in the *better* wars, they just choose the category king—or the lowest price if there's no clear king. A great POV takes you outside the *better* wars and sets you in a *different* space all your own.

A well-executed POV gives the company an identity and culture. It becomes the invisible hand that guides your priorities. It results in the right kinds of employees joining the company, the right kinds of investors funding it, and the right ecosystem building out around it—and, by the way, repels those you don't want hanging around. Ultimately, the POV steers the company's strategy. A powerful POV guides every decision the leadership team makes and every initiative it pursues. The POV helps employees intuitively feel how they should perform their jobs so they align with the company's strategy. Most great, enduring companies have a POV imprinted on their DNA.

Marc Benioff, as described earlier, built Salesforce.com on one of the great technology POVs of all time. In an era of big software and the first fuzzy glimmers of cloud computing, Benioff articulated that Salesforce meant "the end of software." It was different. It was provocative. It challenged the establishment. It put Salesforce on a mission to save customers from the alleged nightmares of traditional business software. It won the company attention from the media. Beyond just the "end of software" slogan, Benioff constructed a deeper POV about how Salesforce was different. It would devote 1 percent of equity to charity and was intent on pushing for a new kind of corporate responsibility. It would speak out on social issues. It would be the industry pirate and defy convention. "A company can't own its facts," Benioff recalled about those decisions. "What a company can own, however, is a personality." And that personality drives action. "We act the way people expect us to, which has made them feel connected to us," Benioff wrote. "It's an emotional attachment, and that's an asset that cannot be stolen by any competitor."[4] To put an exclamation point on that, years later—in 2015—when the state of Indiana passed legislation seen as discriminating against the gay population, Benioff took a highly publicized stand and pulled Salesforce out of the state. The move seemed authentic and not a stunt because it *was* authentic. It fit with Salesforce's long-held POV on the world, and in the end boosted Salesforce's reputation in the tech industry.

Apple under Steve Jobs developed a powerful POV around beautiful design, user experience, and seamless interconnection between various Apple devices, services, and software. Once that POV was established, when Apple came out with new products like the iPhone and iPad, the announcements engendered a feeling of: *of course* Apple would do that. When companies have a strong POV, their actions always seem inevitable.

GoPro built an entire business phenomenon on a *different* point of view. In fact, a big part of its POV was what it called "point-of-view video." Nick Woodman, a surfing nut, cobbled together a rugged waterproof video camera that he could strap onto his body to capture point-of-view video of each awesome wave he caught. When he launched GoPro in 2004, the standard video camera market had become tired and boring. The GoPro camera, Woodman insisted, wasn't different just because it was wearable—it was different because it embodied an adventurous, risk-taking, X Games type of attitude. The people who bought GoPro cameras felt like they became part of the culture, and soon GoPro owners were posting videos online and building an audience. By 2012, GoPro was selling more than 2 million cameras a year while user videos were generating hundreds of millions of views on YouTube. "They've quickly monopolized the idea in a way Band-Aid or Q-tip has where everyone refers to these types of shots as GoPro shots or expect it must've been shot with one," said surfing superstar Kelly Slater, who ended up getting sponsored by GoPro.[5] You know you're the category king when the brand becomes synonymous with the category. GoPro had turned into the category king of a new category of cameras and content. Sony and other big electronics companies tried and failed to compete in the space. They may have built better cameras—in fact, GoPro's cameras were comparatively hard to use—but these competitors had no POV. They had no connection to the target market. In 2014, GoPro went public, and the stock shot up more than 100 percent in a few days, valuing the company at $3 billion. By late 2015, GoPro slumped as its initial category started to run out of potential, and GoPro was slow to expand its potential market. It's yet to be seen how things will turn out for the company.

In our careers, we've felt the power of a great POV. As described earlier, Al, Christopher, and Dave together helped develop a new category and POV for Macromedia in the early 2000s, building the POV around "Experience Matters," experience design, and a new set of Rich Internet Applications products. The POV told the Experience Matters story, and guided Macromedia's strategic decisions. When Dave and Christopher were at Mercury Interactive, they helped reposition the company into a new category with the "Business Technology Optimization" (BTO) POV. When Hewlett-Packard purchased Mercury for $4.5 billion in 2006, the head of HP's enterprise division, Ann Livermore, said that BTO was half the reason HP bought the company.

We're not resolutely stating that no company ever succeeds without a strong POV. Safeway and United Airlines are giant corporations, but they have no POV and sure as hell aren't category kings, so they chug along on low margins and unexciting stock prices and probably suck the souls out of most of the people who work there.[6] Then there's Twitter—a different kind of POV story. Back in 2008, when Twitter first exploded onto the scene, Kevin interviewed cofounder Ev Williams onstage at a Churchill Club event in Silicon Valley, and asked Williams how he'd describe the vision and strategy of Twitter. "I have a sense for what will take off and why and it's mostly gut so I'm not good at articulating it necessarily," Williams responded. "Jack [Dorsey] and Biz [Stone], my other cofounders, have always had grand visions for Twitter. There's a shared sense in the company that we're connecting people and we hear daily how we're changing how people communicate. It's sort of something we feel through osmosis."[7] Translation: We have no POV. We have no strategy. We're watching what our users do and just winging it. (And, by the way, that's been the perception of Twitter ever since.) Twitter got lucky. It created the right thing at the right moment and won the lottery. You, too, can hope you get lucky. We're saying that developing a POV is another important step toward improving your odds of success. It's a way to improve the chances that your initial insight will turn into a company, product, and category that matter.

In the 2010s, we ran across an enterprise-focused company that thoroughly understood category king strategy: Tableau Software, a "visual analytics" company based in Seattle. Tableau deployed a POV that was less in-your-face than Salesforce's "end of software," but the subtlety fit better with the company's chill academic personality.

Tableau's story began with a Stanford University[8] professor, Pat Hanrahan, and his Ph.D. student Chris Stolte researching ways to explore and analyze data by turning the information into interactive visual graphics. As their work progressed, the Stanford guys linked up with Christian Chabot, who had been a data analyst, entrepreneur, and VC, and the three started Tableau in 2003 based on the Stanford research.

From the beginning, the trio believed they could offer something different from what came before. The enterprise market already had lots of "business intelligence" software products, analytics engines, and reporting packages. These products typically cost tens of thousands or even hundreds of thousands of dollars and were only used by specialists who sat through weeks of training to figure them out. The products did important work for companies, pulling together large data sets and mining them for insights. But the products had somewhat the same problem as Siebel's CRM software: they cost too much and were too hard to implement and use. Tableau saw a from/to in the making. It could take enterprise customers from expensive and complex products to much more visual, simple, elegant software. More significant—taking a cue from Salesforce's playbook—Tableau could move a broader set of the population from having zero access to data analytics (because it was too expensive and complex) to being able to use this kind of technology for the first time. "We reinvented the category as something much more broadly applicable and more important for the world," Chabot told us, stating the essentials of Tableau's POV. "It's business analytics software for people who are merely curious or bright and want to see and understand data."[9]

As Tableau refined its POV, it realized it had to evangelize a story that the world had never before heard. It had to convince people who were not data experts that they could get their hands on powerful, easy-to-use analytics. It also had to evangelize the problem Tableau would solve. It had to explain how data could help people understand their jobs and lives better. The Tableau POV—stating that it was marketing a new kind of visual analytics software for people who never knew they needed visual analytics software—drove key initiatives at the company. Chabot noted that it was hard to explain Tableau and its benefits in words, so the company offered a fully functioning free trial—something new to analytics at the time. That way, a broad set of people could try the product. Then Tableau went a step further and developed Tableau Public, a free cloud-based version of Tableau, so even more people could experiment with the technology. Early on, Tableau started a user conference to help its fans share ideas and spread the word. The first took place in a boutique Seattle hotel and drew 50 people. In 2015, about 10,000 showed up at the conference, this time in Las Vegas. As we said earlier, enterprise categories take longer to ramp up than consumer categories, and Tableau's visual analytics needed a good decade to really get going. But by 2014 Tableau was on fire. It reached $400 million in revenue, went public, and became the undisputed category king of this new visual analytics category. The key all along was adopting and holding true to a unique point of view, and letting it seep into every aspect of the company's operations.

We want to acknowledge, though, that a POV is not a new phenomenon. A unique POV was the magic potion that gave wings to mobile computing back in the 1990s. In fact, Palm Computing founder Jeff Hawkins pulled off one of the great POV redirects of all time.

At the start of the 1990s, lots of entrepreneurs, investors, and big companies were chasing the idea of a small, portable digital device. Hawkins worked at one of those companies, GRiD Systems, which developed the GRiDPad. Others in the space included a company called GO, which created the EO; Japan's Casio, which made the Zoomer; and IBM and BellSouth, which teamed on something called Simon. Somewhere in there, Apple (in its Dark Ages era of Steve Jobs's exile) worked on the Newton. All of those devices were disasters. The technology just wasn't available to make a good, stand-alone, handheld device. The products all cost too much (the Zoomer, one of the cheapest, clocked in at $700) and did too little (as in: almost nothing of value). This "personal digital assistant" category—ill-defined and out of synch with its time—was dying. Hawkins was almost a victim. In 1992, he left GRiD to start a company called Palm Computing to make software for various handhelds, and the fading category was taking Palm down with it. If the hardware wasn't selling, there would be no market for software.

The legendary VC who backed Palm was Bruce Dunlevie of Benchmark Capital. With Palm running out of options, Dunlevie met with Hawkins and challenged him to save Palm by making the hardware consumers would actually want. That night, Hawkins sat down and wrote the beginnings of a unique point of view. The device, he wrote, had to cost less than $300 and fit in a shirt pocket. But the most radical idea was that it would be an accessory to a personal computer, not a stand-alone computer. It would synch with a PC so you could walk around with your calendar, address book, and notes, while leaving other files and functions on the host computer. (Keep in mind that Bell Labs first demonstrated wireless Internet access in 1994, so Wi-Fi wasn't available when Hawkins was working on this.) The goals were "hardly revolutionary, yet they were utterly contrary to how the companies in the handheld industry defined their products," wrote Andrea Butter and David Pogue in *Piloting Palm*.[10] Hawkins's POV also forced a critical decision at Palm. To hit his targets for cost, size, and simplicity, Palm needed a new way for people to input information. At the time, the computing power needed to recognize a person's handwriting couldn't be built into a cheap, keyboardless, pocket-size device. So Hawkins came up with the unique solution of teaching human users a kind of shorthand script that the device could more easily comprehend. He called the script Graffiti. In other words, Hawkins concluded it would be easier to teach humans to alter their method of writing than to teach a computer to recognize every handwriting style.[11]

As Hawkins and his team developed the device, the team refined the POV and made it explicit. They wrote it down. "Most competition believes the reason these devices are not selling is the lack of appropriate features," the POV said. "Palm believes the reason they aren't selling is the devices aren't simple enough."[12] Palm even redefined the PDA category, instead calling it "connected organizers." When Palm's engineers pressed Hawkins to add features to the device that would increase its cost or size, Hawkins referred back to the POV and held fast.

Palm launched the Palm Pilot at a demo conference in 1996. The press immediately picked up the story. Word of mouth spread like crazy. Palm also recognized that it had to aggressively spread its antithetical story, so it educated the market with infomercials and public relations efforts. By sticking to the POV, Palm got the product right, and convinced the market the product was right. People accepted Hawkins's aha and saw the problems of cost and uselessness inherent in other handhelds, effectively moving the market from a previous belief to Hawkins's belief. For the first time, a handheld digital device caught on with the mass market, and Palm paved the way for the smartphones we hold dear today.

Timing in a POV Is . . .
Well, Not Everything, but Close

A great POV is not just the right story—it's the right story for its time. The POV has to take into account the state of technology and the mindset of society. An entrepreneur might have a brilliant vision that's exactly right for a decade from now. If that entrepreneur expresses a decade-out POV today, it might get press attention, but it might not feel right to customers. A great POV pushes people just enough into the future, while giving the world a view toward what lies beyond. If the POV sits too much in the present, then at best it's not very exciting, and at worst it makes you seem like a me-too copycat. Cast the POV too far forward ahead of the technology and your team can struggle to make a product that lives up to the promise, while your external audience either isn't ready for your vision or flat-out doesn't believe it.

From our careers, we know what it's like to get the timing right—surfing the perfect wave—and what it's like to misjudge timing, blow the takeoff, and get held underwater for way too long. During the dot-com boom, Christopher was the founding chief marketing officer at Scient. He helped the company come up with a well-timed POV. All sorts of companies in the 1990s suddenly realized they had to have a website, and lots of consultants popped up to help do that. IBM had just begun promoting the concept of eBusiness. Bob Howe, Scient's CEO, had a hunch eBusiness might work as a concept but he, Christopher, and the rest of the Scient founding team also believed that IBM wouldn't be able to execute on the idea in the consulting market. So Scient christened itself the eBusiness "system innovator," launching a new category in the consulting space. The POV perfectly nailed the timing, and Scient became the category king. At three years old, the services firm had a $9 billion market capitalization, then turned into a supernova for the duration of those dot-com boom years.[13]

Al experienced the good and bad of timing, as we've noted earlier in the book. During those same dot-com years, Al founded and built Quokka Sports. His vision for immersive sports over the Internet was exactly right—and its POV made others in the sports industry get the same aha that Al had. NBC signed up Quokka to

bring immersive sports to the Olympics. Yet ultimately Quokka
was too far ahead of technology—its offering didn't work too well
over slow modems, and broadband took longer to get into homes
than anyone had thought. Quokka didn't muster enough momentum to survive the dot-com crash of 2000, and neither did Scient,
showing that even if you get the POV and everything else pretty
much right, timing can kill you.[14]

Reed Hastings of Netflix is truly one of the masters of timing.
He cofounded the company in 1997, and always said he chose the
name Netflix for a reason. He understood that someday the company would offer movies that could be watched directly through
the Internet. But he also knew that the technology would not
be ready for years. He didn't even bother to dangle a streaming-
movie POV in front of the public back in those days. Instead, he
crafted a POV for the times. The concept of choosing your movies on a website and getting DVDs through the mail jumped
just enough into the future, past Blockbuster and its stores and
VHS tapes, but avoided asking consumers to do something they
wouldn't understand. Hastings waited, in fact, until a number of
inconvenient and ill-timed services attempted delivering online
movies—each failing to make an impact. At a conference called
Web 2.0 in 2005, Hastings was interviewed onstage and asked
why Netflix hadn't started streaming movies. He had to explain
why the market wasn't ready, saying the software and antipiracy
mechanisms still presented too much of a hassle for mass-market
users.[15] Netflix in 2007 finally introduced a new POV that set
up a new category of simple, low-cost streaming movies. The
company already had 4.2 million subscribers for its DVD service that he could address, and broadband Internet was rapidly
spreading to U.S. homes. Hastings brilliantly played timing to
make Netflix the category king of two successive categories: first,
DVDs by mail; then streaming movies.

Expressing Your POV

Maybe you're a Steve Jobs or Jeff Bezos or Reed Hastings, and well-crafted, perfectly timed category stories effortlessly spring from your brain. But if you're a little more mortal than that, we propose that you work through a process to help discover and tell a strong story. That process is anchored in the work to discover the category, as described in the previous chapter. By the time you go through those steps to discover the category, you've already identified why the category should exist, and why your company or entity can and will be its king. The POV is a way of expressing that discovery—of telling the story of the category and your role in it.

We can't emphasize enough how important it is to write down this story. A lot of founders and CEOs have a POV in their heads—and then it stays there, expressed only when they speak, leaving others on the team to try to interpret the POV for themselves. All of the pieces of category design work together, and so all the pieces have to be explicit and exact, fitting flawlessly as if in a well-honed machine. Everyone in the organization has to work from the same exact POV. And the only way that will happen is if the POV is written down, massaged, reworked, and fought over until a rock-solid version gets agreed upon by the leadership team. Anyone who rejects the POV at that point is a Zed, and must be removed.

When we tackle this step of expressing the POV, we approach it as if we are creating a movie trailer for the category story. It has to tell the story at a simple gut level. In as few words as possible, it should lay out the problem and its ramifications, describe a vision for the category, sketch a blueprint for how to build the category, and paint a picture of potential outcomes. The strategic use of language matters. A demarcation point in language creates a demarcation point in thinking, which creates a demarcation point in behavior . . . which creates a demarcation point in spending. In order to charge five dollars for a coffee and convince people to wait in a ten-minute line to get it, Starbucks had to call it something different—like a triple grande non-fat latte.

Crafting a POV is a much more serious endeavor than thinking up the classic "elevator pitch," which tries to simplify a company's proposition down to a thirty-second burst. The POV is an articulation of strategy, and has to be solid enough to drive everything else the company does. Far down the line, a company might give some junior communications person the task of crafting a shorter, punchier version of the POV for that rare and coveted occasion when one of the company's leaders happens to ride in an elevator with a potential buyer.

Finding the story can be fun, creative, and at the same time grueling work. We usually grind through a dozen revisions of these documents before they're ready to be shared. And then we think it is best to reveal the trailer at a dinner event that includes the executives, leaders, and key board members involved in the interviews.

That's what we did at Origami. If you recall, the team at Origami ended up landing on the category of Marketing Signal Measurement, identifying a new "thing"—marketing signals—that every marketer needs to measure and understand. But remember, too, that Origami identified a problem that most marketers either didn't know they had or didn't know they could solve. Potential customers needed to be guided from their old way of thinking to Origami's new way of thinking. The POV would be an important step toward conditioning the market—not to mention Origami's employees, investors, and partners—to embrace Origami's insight.

Here was the scene of the debut of Origami's POV: Picture dinner at a rustic, very French restaurant in Menlo Park, California, with the executive team.[16] Everyone has been engaged in category conversations and workshops for weeks, inching closer and closer to category discovery and a category story. Finally everyone gets to see the results together. A screen lights up and a slide show begins.

The slides show stark white words on a black background. The slides—the ones actually shown at the Origami meeting—were sequenced like this, one slide at a time:

- *Do you know what happened today?*
- *It's a simple, powerful question.*
- *That no one in marketing can answer.*
- *Because marketing has become a complex, rapidly changing, noisy, daily battle.*
- *They said modern marketing was going to be easy to measure.*
- *But the explosion of new channels, platforms, apps, devices, data, and the cloud, coupled with the velocity of change . . . has made cutting through the noise almost impossible.*
- *And by 2017 digital will be 40 percent of marketing media spend.*
- *Making measurement a big marketing problem.*
- *As a matter of fact, CMOs report that quality, quantity, and analysis of data is a top concern.*
- *And that measuring consumer engagement across paid, earned, and owned media is a strategic priority.*
- *But, in spite of all of the spreadsheets, agency reports, marketing automation, data warehouses, BI, and CRM, marketing leaders still don't know . . .*
- *What happened today.*
- *UNTIL NOW.*
- *Introducing . . . Marketing Signal Measurement.*
- *Where some see campaigns, channels, devices, and user interactions, we see marketing signals—everywhere.*
- *Signals from every ad, tweet, post, keyword, video play, photo view, blog, app, email, website visit, and offline media execution that matters.*
- *We convert massive streams of marketing signals into actionable marketing insights.*
- *Empowering marketers to measure, analyze, and act on marketing signals. Every day.*

- *Optimizing marketing results. Every day.*
- *And you can also measure your competitors' marketing signals. In real time.*
- *Inciting the curious to know what happened and why.*

By that point, you have the story. It's not about the technology or the product features, even though Origami began with a technology insight. It's not about which company is the best or cheapest. It's also not a steaming pile of business jargon diarrhea, which frankly is the way many corporations express themselves. The story simply and clearly defines the problem and creates a "thing" that modern marketers will feel they must have. That thing is not Origami per se—it's Marketing Signal Measurement. MSM! Origami first needs its potential market to say, "We gotta get that thing!" Once people decide they need MSM, Origami stands a good chance of winning those customers as long as it builds a product that solves the problem well enough. If analysts, journalists, and bloggers understand the category story, they too will describe this new thing, and describe it in the way Origami describes it—which is tied back to the way Origami can solve the problem.

If the world accepts the story and the problem the way Origami laid it out, Origami will always be at an advantage—because the story and problem are tailored to Origami. When all of this works the way it's supposed to work, a category is born, and a probable category king is already on its way to claiming its crown.

POV in Action

Let's say you've debated, teased out, refined, and written down your point of view. Here's how to put that POV to work for the company.

HIRING:

Let your POV help you find the right people and reject the wrong ones. Peter Thiel discovered how that can work when he was building PayPal. "You'll attract the employees you need if you can explain why your mission is compelling: not why it's important in general, but why you're doing something important that no one else is going to get done," Thiel wrote in *Zero to One*. "At PayPal, if you were excited by the idea of creating a new digital currency to replace the U.S. dollar, we wanted to talk to you; if not, you weren't the right fit."[17] Create a clear and compelling POV, and potential employees will self-select to come to you.

INVESTORS:

In 1998, when Amazon.com was preparing for its IPO, Jeff Bezos drafted an initial letter to shareholders that laid out Amazon's point of view. Amazon was still a narrowly focused online retailer, but Bezos made it clear that the company was built for aggressive expansion aimed at the long term. "We will make bold rather than timid investment decisions," Bezos wrote, repeatedly using the word *bold* throughout the POV. And then Bezos treated the POV like holy scripture, re-releasing the letter with every annual report. As a result, Amazon got the right kind of investors and kept out the wrong investors. Amazon's investors knew they were buying stock not in a company that was going to care about quarterly profits, but in one that was going to reinvest in growth and show nary a profit. Without a clear, thoroughly communicated POV, Bezos might have wound up with investors who pressed him to boost profits and cut investment.[18] Whether you're a tiny start-up seeking angel money, a growing company going for a B round, or an IPO candidate, a POV will be the best investor relations tool you'll ever have.

EMPLOYEE ALIGNMENT:

A POV tells employees how to act and guides their decisions. Everything a company does, day in and day out, should align with the point of view. If the POV is clear and employees buy into it, the company will practically manage itself. But that doesn't mean you can just post a POV on your website and expect it to work. Leadership has to evangelize the POV internally. When Dave and Christopher were at Mercury, they helped implement a training program to certify the entire sales force on their ability to deliver the POV. The head of U.S. sales, Joe Sexton, flew around the country personally giving the thumbs up or down as salespeople gave the POV pitch in front of their peers. It sent a clear message. Salesforce.com understands this as well as any company. Early on, the company produced a two-sided laminated card that stated Salesforce's POV along with quick takes on the benefits of its service and other bits about the company. "The card would have been of little use if we had simply distributed it," Marc Benioff wrote. "Instead, we offered training to make sure that everyone was crystal clear on the message that we wanted delivered to the world." He added: "The ultimate result of this meticulous coordination is that everyone is on message with the precision of a sophisticated political campaign."[19] The way you use language recasts thinking, and when you recast thinking, you recast action.[20]

PRODUCT DEVELOPMENT:

A strong POV tells the engineers, product managers, writers, architects, designers, and other creators what to build—and, more important, what not to build. Every product and feature needs to align with the POV and further the company's mission. Apple may be the best example of this in technology. The company is famous for its focus, producing a limited set of products and making sure each aligns with and carries out Apple's point of view on the world. Jobs's other company, Pixar, similarly uses a powerful

POV to guide all its creative decisions. "Our mandate was to foster a culture that would seek to keep our sight-lines clear," CEO Ed Catmull wrote. "The first principle was 'Story Is King,' by which we meant that we would let nothing—not the technology, not the merchandising possibilities—get in the way of our story."[21] By adhering to "Story Is King" and similar principles, Pixar produced one highly praised feature after another. When filmmakers were in doubt about what to do, they knew to default to the Pixar POV. The POV is not a way to describe your products; it's a way to make sure your products are great.

BRAND:

Some cranky business butt-head might hear about POV and grumble that it's the same thing as stuff like branding and positioning. But POV is an articulation of strategy, and so POV *informs* branding and positioning. POV first is the company's identity, looking inward. Once that identity is embraced internally, then the company can turn to the public and confidently say, this is who we are and why we matter. The result is a brand that's more than idle words or a Mike Tyson face tattoo. And when the brand and message are authentic—tied deeply to a company's identity and strategy—the world will take notice. Press, customers, competitors, analysts, and investors can smell authenticity from a mile away. Too many companies have a slogan or tagline that is not grounded in a POV, so it becomes a throwaway line that makes little impact on the company's success. The typical slogan is more forgettable than a deep cut on a Nickelback album and could be used by almost any other company. Witness SAP's "Run simple," or Microsoft's "Where do you want to go today?" Both are POV-free and mean nothing.

To illustrate the impact of a POV on brand and message, let's turn to a moment in Dave's past, when he was hired by software firm Coverity to discover its category, develop a POV, and position the company in the public's mind. Founded in 2002, Coverity was yet another company that grew out of computer science research at Stanford.[22] It was in the business of "static code analysis," the technical term for the process of finding bugs in the software code that runs anything from the Mars Rover to defibrillators or the Android phone in your pocket. By 2008, Coverity was considered the leader in this category, yet the category was nearly invisible—noticed only by the kind of technical people who wore the thickest glasses. Coverity was solving a problem that kept planes from crashing and made sure more than 1 billion devices ran smoothly, but its category story was so buried in the basement of development that most of the world didn't understand the problem Coverity solved, or understand the value of solving that problem. Dave was hired in 2008 as chief marketing officer to fix that.

With Dave's help, Coverity discovered its POV—its true self. That POV revolved around the idea of software integrity. That's what Coverity was about, and the company told the story to potential business customers that the integrity of your software is the integrity of your business. Coverity would explain: Look, a jet airliner has more than 100 million lines of software code, and it's probably a good idea to test it to make sure it all works the way it's supposed to. The company made a case that software integrity testing was a responsibility, not a feature. The Coverity team launched software integrity POV as an advocacy campaign to free the world of software bugs, and the POV helped the company grow more than 20 percent a year and win a position as the clear leader. Analysts ranked Coverity higher than huge incumbents such as IBM and HP. The POV paid off a couple of years later, in 2010, when Toyota Prius cars were being investigated for a potential software glitch that could cause some of them to spontaneously accelerate when the brakes were applied. This software integrity problem resulted in a $4 billion loss in market cap for Toyota. Media outlets contacted Coverity for comments about software integrity, and Dave wound up debating software integrity with automotive gurus on CNBC. All that attention grew out of the POV work and Coverity quickly moved from the development basement to getting heard in boardrooms.

In the end, point of view is an articulation of strategy. If you know and internalize a POV, you have your strategy—that grand overarching plan for creating a category, a company, and a product that matter. But getting to that POV takes a deep mining of the company's soul. The work can take time, and it's hard. But we promise you, it's worth it. Technologists tend to want to build products and figure the rest out later. That's backward. In the next chapter, we'll explain how the best category kings use POV to design a great product, company, and category at the same time. If you still think business is just "make shit and sell shit and everything else is bullshit" . . . if you still think the company with the best product wins . . . if you still think marketing is what you do when you have a shitty product . . . well, good luck with the lottery you're about to enter.[23] If you want to connect your products and company to your category and improve your odds of becoming a category king . . . the next chapter awaits.

The Play Bigger Guide to Point of View Discovery and Expression

Step One: Who?

Point of view development is intricately tied to category discovery and expression. In the previous chapter, we recommended that the category work is best done by someone who is outside of the company's day-to-day operations, yet has the full trust and backing of the CEO and leadership team. Whoever does that work should do this work.

Step Two: Fact Finding

This is another reason to have the same person or team do the category work and the POV work: all of the research needed for category discovery also feeds into the POV work. Please refer back to the end of chapter 4 for the fact-finding questions that need to be addressed. However, for the POV, the team needs to dive into strategic and cultural questions. These should be asked of the founding team and key leaders. The POV is an articulation of the company's strategy and needs to reflect the company's identity, so some of the topics that need to be addressed during interviews include:

HOW THE COMPANY AND PRODUCT ARE DIFFERENT:

The POV needs to express *different*, not *better*. So what is that difference? What are all the things that are different about this company and product? Which ones will strike a chord with which audiences? What is the *different* that could ultimately give the company its identity?

HOW THIS COMPANY WILL CREATE THE PRODUCT OR SERVICE THAT SOLVES THE CATEGORY'S PROBLEM:

Discuss not just what you'll ultimately offer to customers, but how you can get there. What's the road map for achieving the vision? For getting to *different*?

THE ENVISIONED ULTIMATE OUTCOME:

If the company is successful, what will the world look like? How will it be changed? Will it mean, as Salesforce's POV said, "the end of software"? Will it mean, as Sensity forecasted in its POV, the establishment of a new kind of Light Sensory Network? How is that ultimate vision different or the same compared to visions already circulating?

THE NATURE OF THE COMPANY:

Benioff set up Salesforce as a pirate competitor with a humanitarian heart. Southwest has a freewheeling, fun-loving image. Apple is on a mission to bring elegant and uncompromising design to technology. What is your company's culture? What kinds of people lead it? What image does it want with the public and in the media?

Those are squishier questions than those necessary for category discovery, but the POV is as much emotional as it is factual. The research needs to gather as much emotional detail as possible along with the facts.

Step Three: Agree on the Problem

You have to know how to clearly state the problem you're solving before you can describe your solution. Macromedia stated that a bad Internet experience equaled bad business, so bad experiences need to be addressed (by Macromedia's products, of course). Sensity is showing cities that old streetlights are dumb, wasteful, and a problem to be fixed. Origami is saying that marketers don't know what happened today.

Remember what we said earlier: whoever frames the problem best has the best chance of winning the category. Understanding the customer's problem lets loose oxytocin in their brains, opening them up to your way of thinking. So figure out your category's problem, and find a way to say it in a way that touches people's emotions.

Step Four: Craft a Story, Rinse, Repeat

As we said earlier, when we craft a POV, we keep in mind the pacing and emotional tautness of a movie trailer. In a limited number of powerful words, the POV should lay out the problem and its ramifications, describe a vision for the category, sketch a blueprint for how to build the category, and paint a picture of potential outcomes.

The basic structure is much like a classic late-night infomercial. Set up the problem with a dramatic flourish, then describe the solution. We're constantly amazed how many companies market a so-called solution in the absence of a problem. The initial purpose of the POV is to condition the market to understand the problem and demand a solution. The bigger, more urgent, and more strategic the perceived problem is, the more time, attention, and money people will spend to solve it. At the end of the POV, simply describe your company's particular solution in a broad, visionary way. *At no point should a POV get into product features.*

Keep it simple. Use human words, not business or technology words. Keep sentences and phrases short. Be provocative. Think movie trailer!

Make it emotional. Make people feel they must have this. Make them fear not having it.

Paint a vision for the future. This vision will give the audience a sense of where you are going and why they should ride along with you. The vision will also guide the company, its strategy, and its culture. The vision will create a shared sense of mission for employees, customers, partners, investors, and everyone else in the ecosystem.

Inject the POV with the company's personality. Language matters. Should it sound serious and reasoned? Provocative? Aggressive? Playful? Sensity in its POV wanted to make fun of standard streetlights. Part of the POV said, "Don't blame them for being dumb . . . they're just built that way." The approach makes Sensity seem forward-thinking and willing to challenge convention. Origami's language is more sober, reflecting a thoughtful solution to an intractable business problem. In each case, the language signals something about the company culture.

Write the POV as a short document or series of slides. It must be able to be quickly read or presented—perhaps taking no more than ten minutes to absorb. Keep in mind that the Declaration of Independence, one of the most enduring and successful POV documents in history, contains 1,337 words. So there is no excuse for ever writing anything longer than that.

Once a draft is written, present it to the leadership team. Ask for feedback. Take copious notes. Refine the words. Share again. Repeat until the leadership team completely buys into the POV. The team must feel that the POV captures and articulates the category, company, and product strategy, because once accepted, the POV will guide those three things.

Once adopted, the POV can't be altered by different departments for their own needs. Treat it like a hit song you just recorded. Bruce Springsteen doesn't go around changing the lyrics to "Born to Run." So don't change the words of your POV.

Step Five: Distribute, Evangelize, Mobilize

A POV does no good sitting static on a Web page or orphaned on someone's hard drive. Salesforce made laminated cards to give to every employee. Some companies present a POV at an all-hands event, or smaller team meetings. Don't just send it out in a cc:all email. A POV has to be actively evangelized by the CEO and her leadership team.

Train your people in orientation meetings. Certify them. Make it religion. Make it conditional for employment. One very effective training technique is having every new employee stand in front of the entire company and recite the POV. Make it a contest and reward the best presenters. Make it fun and part of your culture.

Invite your people to craft videos and presentations on why the
POV matters. Enlist them and your teams will reward you with
enthusiasm. Also, the Zeds will flee the building.

Once the POV gets injected into the company, use it as the
vehicle to mobilize the company to design and develop the category, company, and product necessary to turn the company into a
category king. How do you do that? Turn the page . . .

6

Mobilization: The Shit Gets Real Chapter

Reality Bites

We want to talk to you about a business phenomenon we call gravity—and how category design works as an antidote to the gravity that pulls a company toward perfectly rational decisions that ultimately end up working against the company's chances to become a category king.

If you want to know the right time to get serious about category design, it's usually when the forces of gravity grow strong. It's one thing to discover and define your category and craft a brilliant POV, but quite another to unleash that work on the company, where it will have to battle gravity day by day, minute by minute. This is where category design gets hard. This is where the shit gets real. This is where category kings are made or ruined.

We know how the dynamic works because we've been in the middle of it so many times, as operators and as coaches or advisors. What we're going to describe in this chapter might sound like it leans heavily toward start-up tech companies, but the same problems and solutions apply to any bold venture led by a mission-driven founder: a new unit inside a big company, a new school or church, a band, a sports league, a nonprofit. The principles are the same, even if the scale and types of forces might be different. We're using enterprise start-ups as a kind of archetype.

When a company gets founded, in most cases the CEO is the
lead product manager. The CEO had the original aha—that initial market or technology insight—and so she establishes true
north for the product, communicating her vision to a small team
through daily conversations and actions, and holding the team
and the product to that vision. Earlier, we discussed the triangle
of product design, company design, and category design, and said
that when all three are in synch, the dynamic boosts the odds
of creating a category king. In the early months of a company,
the typical founder/CEO focuses intently on product design, while
maybe accidentally working on company design and thinking little or not at all about category design. In most cases, that's okay. A
CEO has limited time and mental resources, and devoting them
primarily to product design at the beginning is probably the best
move.

However, as the product gets off the ground and the company
starts to win customers, the CEO gets swept into dozens of other
company-building duties, like sales, hiring, raising money, attending to the board, legal issues, public relations, office space, whether
to bring in donuts on Wednesdays, and on and on. Gravity tugs
the founders (or innovators in a large company) away from working *on* the business toward working *in* the business. This pulls
the CEO away from product design, leaving it to . . . fuck-knows-
who. Maybe no one, because the CEO still thinks she's on top of
the product. Maybe the head of sales starts driving the agenda.
Or a business development guy exerts influence because he claims
he can sign up a couple of "transformative" deals. Those who are
good at spinning or manipulating the CEO will work their spells
through back-channel meetings. Or maybe some poor junior program manager takes the steering wheel because she is the only
person organized enough to build a spreadsheet of all the customer
and partner requests and bug fixes.[1] Whoever it is didn't share in
the CEO's aha, and probably doesn't completely understand the

product's true north. For their own good reasons, they want to tilt the product agenda toward their short-term goals.

After the first customers start using the product, feedback rolls in—user data, ratings, emailed comments, social media comments and tweets, and requests for additional features or functionality. With the CEO busy in the gravitational pull, the junior program manager keeps track of the feedback and things customers are asking for, passing the list on to product managers and engineers. In an enterprise company, the sales force might be out trying to sell everything it can sell, promising potential customers that the company will build whatever the customer wants. The things the customers ask for rarely line up with the true north originally set by the CEO. Instead of working on true north, engineers increasingly find themselves working on customer requests, and customers generally ask for something *better*, not *different*.

This is all acutely true in companies building business products, but it happens with consumer products. Often, it happens much more quickly in consumer companies, since consumers can adopt new technologies, products, and services in an instant. And it can happen very publicly for consumer companies, as the gravity-inducing requests and criticisms pour out into social media.

These forces are the beginning of gravity dragging the product and company away from true north. Pull the product a little off course now and it will continue to veer wildly away from true north over time. Give in to too many custom requests and you wind up with a bag of doorknobs—a bunch of products and features that aren't related and don't add up to a single vision. You wind up building a faster horse instead of Henry Ford's Model T. If you're a founder or CEO and you look at engineering commits for the next Agile sprint and none of what's on there are your ideas, you're in the witching hour of category design—that moment when anything can happen, most likely none of it good.

There are two ways to fight this gravity.

One is to be a maniacal totalitarian visionary product-design asshole.[2] This is how Steve Jobs quite famously and effectively did it.[3] It's why Microsoft was so successful under Bill Gates, and so lost under super sales guy Steve Ballmer, who listened too much to customers, salespeople, and competitors and reacted to what the market was telling him instead of telling the market how to react to him. Few CEOs have it in them to run a company and adhere to true north at the same time.

Given that difficulty, the other way to fight gravity is to set up the POV as true north, and deploy category design as the process that keeps the product, company, and category on track. We've said before that category design involves conditioning the market to see your aha. Well, before you can condition the market, you have to condition your company.

It takes courage to become a category king, and in the witching hour the CEO has to stand behind the POV and category design strategy, and believe in the creation of a new category that doesn't yet exist and can't yet be measured. Gravity doesn't want you to chase a zero-billion-dollar market. Gravity pulls hard toward an existing market that's already defined and that customers already understand. Every business function feels it. An enterprise sales team wants to sell into a line item that exists on their customers' annual budgets, instead of having to convince customers they need a new budget for something they never heard of. Consumer marketers veer toward persuading people to shift their spending to Pepsi instead of Coke, rather than educating them about adding a new kind of item, like a 5-hour Energy shot. Engineers lean toward building a product that's better than others on the market, not different from anything they've seen before. Marketing, finance, PR, HR—they all feel the tug of gravity. Everybody tends to skate to where the puck is instead of to where it's going. And in that moment, it takes courage for the leader to turn away from some giant amount of revenue now because she *just knows* that true north is the right path and that creating, developing, and dominating an entirely new category is the better strategy. Category kings don't ignore *everything* gravity pulls them toward, but they have to find a magical line between giving the market just enough of what it's asking for and leading on to a new place—to a new category of the future.[4]

This battle against gravity is the manifestation of the desperate, palpable, jaw-clenching tension between today's revenue and the future of the company. And while we know it sounds crazy to many, in the category king game you are playing for future economics, not today's revenue. You will have to continually grow the category potential and push the perception that you are the king, following the equation that says a company's value is determined by its category's potential, the company's position in the category, and its ability to prove it can deliver on its promises. Doing that while controlling the forces of gravity yanking on a company can be a lot to ask of many leaders. That's when category design becomes the CEO's ally.

Absent category design, a company gets past gravity and becomes a category king by force of a CEO's personality or sheer dumb luck. Category design improves the odds of any CEO and company fighting off gravity to get to category king status.

Implementing Category Design

The day after the POV is delivered and adopted by the leadership team, it's time to go into execution mode. This is when all the category design work moves away from a select few in the leadership circle and gets injected into every part of the company. When we work with companies, the category discovery and POV are often the fun part, when the leadership team is excited to see us and intrigued by the process. Now comes the work to make the category design stick.

There's a mechanism for making this happen. We call it a lightning strike. (The substance of this chapter and the next chapter actually involve parallel activity, but since this is a book, we have to write about them serially. That's why you'll read some about lightning strikes here and some in the following chapter.) When we work alongside an executive team, right after the POV gets marked "done," Dave chairs a meeting with the leadership team to identify and schedule a lightning strike within three to six months. A lightning strike is an event meant to explode onto the market, grab the attention of customers, investors, analysts, and media, and make any potential competitors crap their drawers. It is the full concentration of the company's resources on one high-intensity strike. This is in complete opposition to traditional peanut butter marketing, which involves spreading marketing and PR across a wide swath of the market over a long period of time and hoping somewhere it sticks. Peanut butter marketing doesn't break through in this era of cacophonous media and never-ending swarms of new start-ups seeking attention.

A lightning strike must overcome the noise. The strike is a shock-and-awe version of what some marketers call "air wars"—the campaign to change potential customers' minds so they consider buying the company's offering. ("Ground wars," in that formulation, usually refers to the more hand-to-hand work of lead generation, sales calls, and closing deals.) Smart companies know they need both air wars and ground wars to move their target's brains so they then move their buying patterns. Lightning strikes get air wars off with a resounding bang.

Some of the best strikes hijack an event, like an industry conference or trade show, where a good number of the target audience will be gathered. Sensity did this at Lightfair International in 2013. Another tactic is to create your own high-profile, heavy-hitter event, perhaps convening thought leaders and potential

customers at a "summit" built around the problem you're going
to solve. The point is to identify the right moment, and think
of the lightning strike in the way Hollywood thinks of opening
weekend for a blockbuster movie: a whole lot rides on it, so go
as big and loud as you can, with the whole company 100 percent
behind the effort.

Why schedule it within months? The pace of category creation
is speeding up drastically. And since one king in a given category
runs away with all the economics, you have to stake your claim
to the crown fast, or risk losing your chance. There is no time to
waste. And three to six months is long enough for a company to
prepare for a strike, and short enough to make everyone focus. We
find that the best work is done fast. If you ever see "version 21"
on any document, you can bet it has been spoiled by too many
revisions over too much time. A tight window also prevents scope
creep and indecision.

The most important thing to understand about a lightning
strike is that it's *not a marketing event*. It's a *company event*. And this
is why the strike becomes a forcing function for every part of the
company. Once the work is done to define the category and set up
the vision, the lightning strike is meant to show the world that
the category and vision are real, imminent, and inevitable. And
to do that, the lightning strike has to introduce the product and
company strategy that will make that POV real, imminent, and
inevitable. The products have to work, make sense, and add up
to a vision and not a bag of doorknobs. Every other function at
the company has to line up behind the POV at the strike. The
sales team must know the use cases and offerings and be able to
sell into the POV. Marketing, branding, visual design, social and
viral growth tactics, and advertising all must be in synch with the
product and POV at the lightning strike. Company strategy and
financial strategy must be in synch with the POV at the lightning

strike. Every employee must understand the POV by the lightning strike and understand how his or her job snaps into the vision for the product, company, and category.

Some other tasks that have to get done in the run-up to the strike include creating new sales decks; writing and producing the lightning strike press materials; updating the brand so it lines up with the POV; preparing analysts so they understand the use cases, company, and category strategy; nailing the growth hacking approaches required to drive digital metrics; and readying the company website so it reflects the POV and takes full advantage of the strike. Workflows can get tricky because of interdependencies— marketing needs to do its job so sales can know how to put together its pitch; product marketing needs to define the use cases so the marketing team can speak to the right audience in the right way; and so on. Because of the tight deadline, everything has to happen almost at once, yet it still has to happen in the right order. Someone inside the company who is respected across departments needs to project-manage the whole affair—and it can be a daunting task. In the end, every company will have a different checklist and process, but the lightning strike becomes the moment when every aspect of category design has to come together as a single whole. And when that happens, a lightning strike can turn into a category king coronation.

And that is why you set a date for a lightning strike right after adopting the POV. As soon as you set that date, the clock starts ticking and a whole set of vectors get set in motion. You are truly *mobilizing* the company. It's like the Allied forces setting a date for D-Day, then working backward and putting in motion everything that has to happen for D-Day to work. And if everything isn't ready and in synch by D-Day, the whole thing will fall apart.

There are a few ramifications that come into play once you set the strike mobilization in motion. In our experience, it almost always creates a shared sense of purpose across the company—a kind of battle-hardened camaraderie. That shared mission smokes out the Zeds in the company. As most of the employees unite behind the POV, it becomes increasingly obvious who refuses to buy in or, worse, fights against the mission. There is no room for Zeds at a company on a march toward a lightning strike. And the work to prepare a strike can actually make employees' lives better. It sets priorities, so it becomes clear what they should work on and what they should ditch. It gives them permission to stop doing stupid shit, because there's just no time. The measure of an employee's value swerves away from the amount of work getting churned out and instead becomes centered on how effectively the work helps the strike be successful.

The CEO has to throw all of her political capital behind the lightning strike. She is the only one who can drive this priority through the entire company. She must not only believe—she must be the chief category officer. If the CEO wavers or hedges or doesn't commit the resources or gives any part of the company permission to deviate from the lightning strike mobilization, the strike will fail.

A Few Things Most CEOs
Never Think of Doing

We're pretty sure that few people reading this have drawn up a blueprint for their category or a taxonomy that names everything for the category, or thought through the category's use cases, or painted a picture of an ecosystem. We'll tell you what that stuff is and why we believe you should do these things in the charge toward the lightning strike. We're not saddling you with a meaningless pile of consultant-y make-work. This is the business equivalent of writing a script and laying out a storyboard for a movie instead of letting everybody improvise. The good news is that much of what you need is probably already floating around the company.

Hopefully this work will capitalize on and amplify work that's already been done but hasn't been assembled in a cohesive manner.

We realize we're going to hit you with a lot of to-dos in these next pages. We recommend you break at some point and open a bottle of something with alcohol in it.

Let's say you've finished your POV and set a date for the lightning strike. As every department starts planning its drive to the strike, the leadership team should sit down and thoroughly imagine the category the company is trying to create. But just imagining the category is not enough. You need to make the implicit become explicit. We recommend creating four seminal documents: a category blueprint, product taxonomy, customer use cases, and category ecosystem. If you're inside a well-funded start-up, the output of this work should look well honed and professional. But a two-person start-up in a backyard shed or an individual designing a career might do this on the back of a napkin. The most important part is that you think these things through and write them down.

Category blueprint: Category kings design the product, company, and category at the same time. The blueprint marks the start of designing the category. If you're different and not just better . . . if you're nonconsensus and hope to flip over to consensus . . . that means your category does not yet exist. You have to invent and design it. And then you have to put it on paper in a way that helps employees, customers, investors, analysts, and the media comprehend how the category should work and what role you'll play in it. Many companies develop a product road map that details how a product will evolve and what its end state might look like. This does something similar, but for the whole category.

The blueprint is a design for how the product or service will work going forward. It should tell customers what they can expect the category king to deliver. A public company can't publish a product road map because it is considered a forward-looking statement. But a category blueprint can and should be an external document. It is meant to show people what to expect over time from the *category*. It's not a promise of what the company will deliver, but a vision of a category that the company wants to bring into existence. An advantage of publishing the category blueprint is that it seeds dread among would-be competitors, who look at the blueprint and think you've already put the whole thing in motion. Microsoft in its heyday was brilliant at this tactic. Just describing where the category of "PC operating system" was heading caused would-be competitors to assume Microsoft would do all that, and many of them would just give up and retire. A category blueprint serves as thought leadership, putting you in position to take a category where you want it to go. One company we know put its category blueprint into its S-1 filing for its IPO. As we said, the company that best describes the category has the best odds of owning it.

Every category's blueprint will be different, and there are many ways to depict them, but the larger point is that the document needs to show an outside audience that you've thought out the category, and that you have a plan to execute. That's an important step toward establishing your company as the leader and most important player in the new category.

PRODUCT TAXONOMY:

The category blueprint often leads to an "oh shit!" moment inside a company. The blueprint paints a picture of what your product needs to become, and then you look back at the current product and suddenly see what's missing, or misrepresented, or packaged wrongly. So you have to sit down and think about the current product through the lens of the blueprint. Maybe you need to pull out features that were buried inside the overall product and give those pieces new names. Maybe you need to split the product into pieces and re-label and re-price them, or put pieces together in a new way. Basically, this exercise means taking your product apart, giving the pieces labels that synch with the blueprint, and putting it all back together so it makes sense for the category you're designing. As you go, you are repackaging and repricing the product as necessary.

The document you create as you do this is called a product taxonomy. Having a common way of describing everything is critical. The taxonomy becomes "truth" and it describes all the elements of the solution and how they fit into the category. Words matter. Category kings lead with language. The name of products and features can change the way people value them. That's why automobile dealers no longer sell used cars. They sell pre-owned vehicles. It was hard for Congress to vote against something called "the PATRIOT Act." If you want the world to value your product innovations, give them innovator names that tie back to your category design.

USE CASES:

As the company works on its product taxonomy, which is a deep inward dive into your offering, a parallel step involves using the blueprint lens to look outward at customers. If the category develops the way you're designing it, how will customers use your product? Classically trained marketers develop use cases as a way to understand who to sell to. In category design, use cases are a way for the entire company to better understand how to design the product and company so they address the needs of the category over time.

Identify who the customers are. And then think through the elements of what makes a great new category. For instance, remember that a new category solves a problem in a new way—so what is that problem and how will you solve it? What is that from/to journey you want to take users through? What's the ultimate benefit? Again, different people around the company have probably already thought about a lot of this. Pull that thinking out of wherever you might find it: sales decks, persona studies, segmentation analysis, marketing work, and so on. The more the use cases can be specific and detailed, the easier it will be for marketing and sales to be effective. Absent use cases, you're doing the equivalent of sending your team out hunting and only telling them they have to come back with food. They won't know where to go or what weapon to take along. Things get easier if they know they're specifically hunting pheasant. Get crisp and get real.

Once again, the point is to think it through and write it down, in whatever format works for you. The very act brings clarity. Use the lightning strike mobilization to force the issues and speed up the work. This can't be a six-month study. In the march toward a lightning strike, the work has to be a fast and furious drive.

CATEGORY ECOSYSTEM:

The blueprint defines the category architecture, the taxonomy describes your product and offer as it relates to the category, and the use cases define the category's customers and pain points. The remaining piece involves the outside players who will be involved in the development of the category. We call this the category ecosystem, and mapping it out completes your understanding of how to develop and dominate your new category.

Every healthy category has a healthy ecosystem around it. The players include third-party developers, consultants who help companies adopt your product, stores that carry a consumer product, analysts, data or content providers, partners of all stripes, and even competitors. Salesforce.com nurtured an enormous ecosystem of people and entities who rely on Salesforce for their commercial well-being. That ecosystem becomes tangible every year when the company's Dreamforce conference draws 150,000 attendees. VMware began working on its ecosystem from early on by creating programs that certified technologists in virtual machine software and building up its VMworld conference, now drawing more than 20,000 ecosystem members a year. The ecosystem for Netflix includes movie studios, original content creators, Internet-enabled TV makers, and the U.S. Postal Service (for delivering DVDs). Clarence Birdseye developed an ecosystem nearly a hundred years ago that included railroad companies, grocers, farmers, and freezer makers.

No company exists in a vacuum. All are surrounded by an ecosystem. A vibrant ecosystem, in fact, needs its category king. If the king falters, the ecosystem can actually help prop it up. The ecosystem fills in the spaces of the category. The combined efforts of the ecosystem act like a multiplier for the category king.

But a category king defines and exerts control over its ecosystem, so everyone plays by the king's rules. That means that competitors in the category wind up having to play by the king's rules, too—a clear advantage for the king. Any ecosystem has control points—places where one entity can exert enormous control. Apple's iTunes serves as a control point for all the media flowing into iPods, iPhones, and iPads. Wal-Mart became a massive control point for hard retail goods flowing to Americans. Bloomberg made itself a choke point for information getting to Wall Street. Control points are a great place to collect tolls and make a ton of money. Hopefully, in designing your category, you own a control point.

For all those reasons, we believe you should think through and explicitly map the category ecosystem you plan to create. If you know what you want it to be, you'll know better how to develop it. And the process of developing your ecosystem needs to start at the lightning strike, so the strike jolts the ecosystem to life.

We believe it's important to tackle these mobilization documents soon after the lightning strike date gets set, because the work can have so many downstream effects. The documents inform the strike and keep everyone on track when gravity bites hard. While the POV sets the tone, it does so at a very high level.

The blueprint, product taxonomy, use cases, and category ecosystem get down into the guts of the company strategy and tactics.

This stage of category design requires challenging thought exercises and decisions. But that's why the process of category design can help. By this point, you've defined your category and composed a POV, which can guide the company's strategy. You've set in motion a lightning strike, which serves as a forcing function to make the company mobilize and get things done. As part of that mobilization, you formulate a series of mobilization documents that help every part of the company see how the category will work and their role in it. All of this is category king strategy made explicit and put in motion.

If you're a leader at a company going through this, you should take care to monitor and understand the deep impact it will have on many employees.

Mobilization can be freeing because it focuses everyone's work on a common goal. In other cases it can make product and engineering teams go psycho. Take care if you need to tell them that their children have to be taller and smarter and have new names. You hopefully are working with some of the brightest engineers in the world, and they have emotional ties and great pride in their work. Respect this and keep it in mind during every meeting.

Also expect some devotees of Agile and Extreme programming to fight back. They will say that their methods are proof a blueprint cannot be defined or delivered. Agile and Extreme are high-speed, short-burst work processes built around quickly designing good-enough products by the end of each work sprint. That often leads to comments like, "We don't plan out six months let alone eighteen months." But category design is a balance between speed and vision. In today's environment, any company can do speed. Category kings harness speed for a larger cause.

Product leaders might argue that the mobilization work will require some phenomenal amount of man-hours and require brutal trade-offs in day-to-day operations. That's human nature. And that's what the lightning strike is intended to combat. When the whole company goes on a three-month race to D-Day, leaders can say that everything that's not serving the strike can wait.

Sales teams can kill a mobilization in their QBRs (quarterly business reviews), Monday morning calls, or a well-timed email to the CFO at the end of the quarter. All they need to do is blame the category work for why a deal slipped through. Company leaders need to understand those tensions and find that magical line between doing what's required in the short term while building the category. In extreme cases some have to sacrifice immediate revenue or margins for future domination.

Gravity is a force that will try to drag down your mobilization every day in every possible way. Walk the line between what's required today and what matters for the future.

If the Suit Fits . . .

The truth lives in the mobilization phase of category design. The leadership can kid themselves about their capabilities, resources, drive, and courage as they discover a category and write a POV. Nobody can hide in a mobilization. Products that don't work, marketing that sucks, an engineering team that's too shallow, sales teams that promise too much, burn rates going too fast—any obstacle to the lightning strike will become obvious now. If the CEO and the board don't have the stomach to create a category that doesn't yet exist—it will become obvious now. If the leadership team has a weak link—it will become obvious now. We've seen many CEOs melt like a Popsicle dropped on a summer sidewalk at this stage. They dilute the whole thing with a week or two to go and end up executing a run-of-the-mill marketing campaign, not a lightning strike.

The big question then is: Does the suit fit? In other words, did you craft a category strategy that fits the company—what we call company/category fit? Maybe the vision is too big, like when an eighth grader wears his dad's suit to a dance. Maybe it's too small. As work toward the lightning strike progresses, you'll know. Given all the dependencies in a run-up to a strike, if there are problem situations, you'll hear it multiple times from multiple sources. Then you have to assess. There will always be problems that arise—but are they problems that can be fixed? Is there just one Zed whom you need to fire and replace with someone better—or are you running into a gang of Zeds who are sabotaging the plan? Can the holes in the product get filled in by a couple of first-class engineers—or did you overshoot what you can possibly build?

We worked with one company, which we won't name, that got to this stage and figured out that the suit was about four sizes too big. They had already crafted a POV and were diving into the mobilization phase. But the CEO could not fight gravity. He too strongly felt the pull of today's market versus tomorrow's market cap. He felt more comfortable with *better* instead of *different*, and so could not get out and authentically evangelize the new category. His teams knew that the CEO's conviction was weak, and that created a wait-it-out syndrome—employees held back, waiting to see if the category design work was really going to get implemented. The rest of the company would not fall in line and get the work done. The company had to downsize its POV—downsizing it to the point where it was all about *better* and just didn't matter to the marketplace. We doubt that company will ever be a category king. And that's okay—not every company can be a king.

There's another possible response to realizing the suit is too big. You might decide the suit is too big *now*, but you can grow into it. You might adjust the POV while keeping the grander vision in your back pocket. Jeff Bezos didn't start Amazon with a POV of becoming the most powerful force in retailing since the rise of Wal-Mart. He started with a POV of becoming the world's biggest bookstore. That was, as he often said, the formulation behind the company's name: the Amazon is the world's biggest river, and Amazon.com would be the world's biggest bookstore. Once Bezos conquered his original POV, he kept instituting more ambitious ones. Early on in the life of Facebook, Mark Zuckerberg would talk about a grand ambition of connecting everyone in the world on his platform, but that suit would've been way too large for the young company. The early POV was built around connecting college students, while Zuckerberg kept the grand vision in his pocket until the time was right to make it the institutional POV.

Hopefully, though, you'll find that your POV fits. You'll undoubtedly have to do some tailoring. You might have to change out a couple of executives or jettison features you can't build in time. You will know the POV is ambitious enough if you feel the stress on the company as it tries to get to the lightning strike. Your chief operating officer might feel like Scotty on *Star Trek*, and run into your office yelling, "She canna take any more, captain! She's gonna blow!" But if you have confidence that the strain is just the result of driving hard, and that your vessel can handle it, then slam the throttle forward and make lightning happen.

Stories of Gravity

To make the subject of gravity less abstract, we have a couple of stories to tell. One we know intimately. It's about the role of gravity in the downfall of Macromedia's Flash multimedia software—a version of the story that probably hasn't been told elsewhere. The other is just a wonderful example of a desperate company overcoming gravity to create one of the great industrial category kings: Chrysler's minivan.

When the consumer Internet first exploded, it could not handle animation let alone audio and video. Modem speeds into homes could barely carry tiny images. In 1996, Macromedia bought an animation company called FutureSplash and developed it into an animated graphics and video tool called Macromedia Flash, and a player, which consumers downloaded onto their PCs, called the Flash Player. The company cut deals to bundle Flash Player software into popular browsers such as Netscape Navigator and Microsoft Explorer, which enabled content owners to use Flash to reach those audiences, which in turn created an industry standard so the bulk of Internet video ran on Flash. "We nurtured the ecosystem so no one else could get in," said Rob Burgess, who was CEO at the time.[5] As broadband spread to homes and offices in the early 2000s, Macromedia became the undisputed category king of Internet video software. Flash became so dominant, it could call the shots with its customers. Owning both the development tool and the player meant Macromedia had the control point and even Microsoft had to play along.

Around 2006, Al was working at Macromedia, which had just been bought by Adobe, when the ground started to shake under digital video. YouTube, founded in 2005, exploded onto the scene. Video had grown on the Web in fits and starts, but YouTube turned it into a runaway train. In July 2006, YouTube announced that 65,000 new videos a day were being uploaded to the site. A few months later, in October 2006, Google bought YouTube for $1.7 billion. YouTube ran on Flash, and suddenly a Google-owned YouTube had enormous clout when it came to things like the software that ran its videos. At the same time, the first smartphones were entering the market and Nokia reigned as the global leader. NTT DoCoMo and KDDI in Japan had pioneered one of the fastest-growing digital ecosystems in the world based on Flash content.[6] Verizon and AT&T Wireless had consolidated much of the power in the U.S. cellular provider market and were focused on delivering an emerging breed of "data services" to these new smartphone owners. In the background, Apple started working on its iPhone, which would be introduced in 2007.

That's when gravity started working on Flash. The proven market was on desktops and laptops, serving video through browsers. A great deal of Macromedia's resources went into developing and selling to that ecosystem. YouTube demanded higher-definition video, so naturally the Flash team went to work on that customer request. The company could see that mobile was taking off, and worked on a light version of Flash (called Flash Lite) that could run on smartphones. Even there, the gravity pulled the work toward the needs of Nokia—the existing power. Verizon and AT&T, which wanted rich media to move over its networks without eating up massive amounts of bandwidth, had requests. Then Steve Jobs marched into Adobe with his plan for the iPhone. Apple had little power to wield at that time and had zero presence in mobile. Jobs demanded that Flash had to work on the iPhone exactly as it worked on a laptop—a very difficult proposition at the time, especially given the limited computing resources on smartphones. The list of requests from all the different customers grew longer and longer. Gravity pulled the team toward today's contracts, commitments, and revenue, which was in many ways the rational decision at the time. In response to Apple's request for help getting Flash running on the prototype iPhone, the company put four engineers on Flash for Apple—a measly amount of resources in retrospect.

Al was part of the Adobe leadership team that decided to bend with the gravity—to allocate the bulk of the resources for Flash to the large existing customers and the next version of Creative Suite and not bet on the iPhone. There are some decisions in business you wish you could redo. This sure was one of them for Al.

As Jobs realized that Flash would not run fast enough on iPhones and consume too much of the iPhone's resources, he turned vicious, famously vowing that Flash would never sully Apple's mobile products. As the iPhone and iPad took wing, minus Flash, power shifted to Apple, and developers and content providers started abandoning Flash. Macromedia, the onetime king, became a victim of gravity—the same kind of gravity that can derail any drive to build and maintain a category king.

Twenty years before the Flash showdown, in the 1980s, Chrysler fought off gravity as it developed one of the most *different* vehicles to come out of Detroit. Actually, before Chrysler, both General Motors and Ford had drawn up plans for a family passenger van that would land somewhere between car and truck, but gravity killed it at both companies. GM decided instead to push resources into developing small cars to compete against the new threat from Japan. (In retrospect, that was a bad category strategy, since Japan by then won category king status in small cars.) At Ford, the leadership flat-out didn't have the guts to evangelize something *different*. Chrysler was able to fight gravity because of two important elements: CEO Lee Iacocca was willing to bet his career on something *different*, and Chrysler was in such bad shape it needed a breakout category-defining success because there was no way it had the resources or time to compete for market share on *better* alone. Basically, Chrysler at the start of the 1980s found itself in the same position as many start-ups today: everything was riding on whether it could define, develop, and dominate a new category. "The company was history in everybody's mind," recalled Glenn Gardner, then an engineer on the minivan project. "We needed a success to stick in everybody's ear."[7]

Using demographic research into the massive Baby Boom generation just moving into parenthood, Iacocca painted a clear picture of the missing category this new vehicle would step into. This served as Chrysler's POV. The minivan had to be positioned as superior to a station wagon, so it needed the comforts and options of a car but the interior space of a truck. Yet the roof had to be low enough to fit into residential garages, and the nose had to be visible from the front seat so suburban drivers could easily park. All of that meant building

a front-wheel drive van—something that didn't exist yet. To build
a vehicle unlike any before it, Chrysler would have to revamp an
entire factory in Windsor, Ontario. It would also need to come up
with unique marketing that fit the POV and train thousands of car
dealers on the new offering, all while keeping the engineers from
compromising or veering away from *different*. The cost of everything
would be staggering—around $700 million in 1980 dollars, or
more than $2 billion in 2015 dollars. Iacocca diverted money from
other programs around the company, turning away from today's revenue because he believed in tomorrow's blowout success. "Iacocca
stood behind it," said Stephan Sharf, who then ran Chrysler's manufacturing operations. "We weren't flush, and there were a lot of other
product requirements."[8]

The pull of gravity was enormous and could've tanked the
strategy. But Iacocca evangelized and pushed the throttle. The rest
of the company bought in. A camaraderie developed, built around
that desire to "stick it in everybody's ear."

Chrysler introduced its minivan line in 1983. It performed the
way a category king performs. Reviewers and buyers quickly understood the "missing" that the minivan solved—how to cart around a
suburban family in style. Sales raced to 190,000 in 1984. Ten years
later, unit sales would hit that number in just three months. The
minivan became its own category, and every major competitor—
GM, Ford, Honda, Toyota—came into the category with a competing product. Every one of those attempts reinforced the appeal of
the category, and the benefits flowed primarily to the king: Chrysler.
Chrysler held on to the vast majority of market share and profits
from the category for the next thirty years. In 2014, Chrysler's two
minivan models—the Chrysler Town & Country and Dodge Grand
Caravan—together accounted for 49 percent of total minivans sold
in the United States. Honda had 23 percent and Toyota nabbed 22
percent, with 6 percent going to other stragglers.[9]

Gravity can be a brutal force. But if you can mobilize a company to beat it, the view from high up is worth the effort.

The Play Bigger Guide to Mobilization

Step One: Who?

Two key actors make mobilization happen.

One is the CEO. No one else can make the entire organization get behind the mobilization effort and march it to the finish line. The CEO must completely believe in the category design plan, evangelize it throughout the company and ecosystem, and stick by it when the shit gets real.

The other is the lightning strike master controller. One person needs to track the entire process and all the dependencies, and sound the alarm when something goes awry. The master controller should not be the CEO (who wouldn't have the time), but needs to have direct access to the CEO. Otherwise, it can be anyone from the leadership team—a CMO, CTO, CFO, etc.

Step Two: Set the Lightning Strike in Motion

Right after adopting the POV, plot a date three to six months out for a lightning strike. Look for an event to hijack, or some other reason to have the strike that day.

Next, decide what the strike will deliver. Who will be targeted? What are the from/tos for each target? (There's much more about this in the next chapter.) What will be unveiled that day, and how? What offerings need to be ready? How will they deliver on the category promise and company POV? Like your own D-Day, schedule the date and plan what's supposed to be accomplished, then work backward to get it all done in time.

Step Three: Mobilize Everyone

Once you know what the lightning strike will deliver, decide what every part of the company has to do to make it happen. Bring every department head into the plan, and set them in motion to carry out their roles. Make sure the spirit of the strike work filters out to every single employee so each person knows his or her role.

At the same time, the CEO needs to look for Zeds and watch for problems that need to be fixed for the lightning strike to work.

Step Four: Draw Up the Four Seminal Mobilization Documents

You are designing a product, company, and category at the same time. This is how you design the category—by making it explicit in category blueprint, product taxonomy, use cases, and ecosystem documents. Use visuals to paint a picture of what the category will look like once you become the category king and solve the problem that the category raises. Think of it more broadly than just your company—think of what it looks like when a healthy category emerges, with you on top. Show it in a way that proves to investors, customers, and competitors that you've thoroughly thought this through and already know how to do it. It will freeze would-be competitors in their tracks.

Step Five: See If the Suit Fits

Mobilization is the phase where truth lives. No one can hide. No problem can be buried. The bare realities of what the company can accomplish become absolutely evident. The CEO needs to pay attention to those signals—and, critically, be self-aware enough to know whether she herself can pull off a category king strategy.

Measure the company's capabilities next to the POV and see if they fit. If the suit is too big, it will be necessary to tailor the suit—scale back the vision captured in the POV.

In some cases, it might become evident that the suit is too small. That means the POV was too cautious. This is the time to decide if the company needs a grander goal.

Step Six: Watch for Trouble

If you hear an engineer say that the mobilization work will take six hundred people-hours—that's engineer code for "Fuck you. We're not doing this."

If the Zed doesn't attend the meeting, he is off doing destructive Zed shit. Saying he wasn't at that meeting and didn't participate in the decision is a typical Zed's excuse for not doing what he's supposed to be doing.

If everybody on the team doesn't know all of the critical deadlines and what they are on the hook for, the mobilization master controller is not being effective.

If the CEO doesn't ask about a strike update in every executive team meeting, then the company is by default running a marketing campaign, not a category-defining strike.

If the board of directors does not know why you are investing in the strike, they are going to pitch a fit when they see how much is being spent on "marketing."

If the sales team members who never had an opinion about marketing start saying customers "don't like the message," those salespeople are already missing their numbers and will try to blame it on the mobilization and strike.

If you are the CEO and see any of the above happening at your company, you need to double down on evangelizing the category strategy.

Step Seven: Get 'er Done

The biggest challenge is getting everyone to the moment of the lightning strike so everything is in place and works as it should. It requires smart management and hard work. Like *Star Trek*'s star ship *Enterprise*, the stresses will increase the faster you go and the closer you get, until it seems like the whole thing is going to blow. Keep going. Keep working. Tie up loose ends. Improvise where you have to. Keep your eyes on true north. And believe that the strike will begin to bend the universe in your direction.

7

Marketing: Conditioning the Market to Welcome Your Pirate Invasion

How to Get Attention

Sensity is the start-up that pulled off a serious pirate move by establishing a new category called the Light Sensory Network, catching giants such as GE, Cisco, and Philips off guard and forcing them to follow and react. In 2013, the phrase "Light Sensory Network" went from zero recognition to global conversation in about a week. That was the week Sensity pulled off a truly legendary lightning strike.

In the previous chapter, we got into how to mobilize a company to prepare for a lightning strike, but we haven't yet described lightning strikes, their impact, and how to vault off of them to build your case to be a category king. That's what we're going to do here, starting with Sensity's story.

As we've been saying, a lightning strike is an all-consuming event, concentrating a company's resources to break through the noise and start to condition the market. Sensity, though, had scarce resources to concentrate. The scrappy start-up had soldiered on for three years under another name, Xeralux, pitching itself primarily as an LED light company. CEO Hugh Martin, however, had much grander plans. He saw how LED lights could be armed with sensors capable of detecting motion, gases in the air, sound, weather, and other factors, turning lights into a distributed data collection system. On a small scale, such data could tell a shopping mall owner when the parking lot got full. On a grand scale, if these lights were deployed globally, they could track human migration patterns or detect earthquakes. This was a far bigger idea than lighting. It was a new category—a convergence of lighting, networking, and data science. Internally, Martin and his team did the work to define the category, calling it a Light Sensory Network, or LSN. They constructed a point of view and changed the company name from Xeralux to Sensity. But then came the big challenge for this pipsqueak and its nonconsensus category: Sensity had to rise above the noise.

In January 2013, Martin and his marketing chief, Amy Lee, circled a date on the calendar: April 23, 2013. That day, the world's lighting makers and their customers would all be in Philadelphia for the annual convention called Lightfair International. That's where Sensity would unleash its strike. If all went well, Sensity, then with forty-three employees, would hijack the convention, using it to turn attention to the emergence of Light Sensory Networks.[1]

The strike was then about four months away, and it acted as a forcing function for mobilization, much as we described in the previous chapter. Martin and Lee courted a few elite reporters, trying to get at least one to write a story about LSN that would appear the day of the strike, which Sensity was billing as its big unveiling. They approached Don Clark[2] of the *Wall Street Journal*, who thought the story was interesting and agreed to hold it for April 23 in exchange for having the story exclusively. Everything seemed to be set up for the Lightfair hijack. And then, as so often happens, events shook up the best-laid plans.

In an unusual twist, Sensity had a connection to the president of El Salvador, Carlos Mauricio Funes Cartagena. When Funes, a former journalist, learned about Sensity and LSN, he told the company he wanted to do a deal that would bring LSN to El Salvador to help with safety issues and with monitoring the nation's ports. He was going to be in Washington, D.C., in mid-April, and proposed a joint announcement with Sensity on April 18. Sensity agreed, realizing the announcement about bringing LSN to El Salvador could be a good prelude to the lightning strike.

Then, on April 15, 2013, two pressure-cooker bombs exploded near the finish line of the Boston Marathon. The brutal act, its aftermath, and the search for the perpetrators riveted the nation and took over the news. At the *Wall Street Journal,* Clark, who had come to understand that Sensity's LSN could detect odd patterns of behavior and might forewarn authorities about someone placing a bomb, decided his LSN story needed to run right away.[3]

So this became Sensity's lightning strike: Clark's *WSJ* story April 16 broke the news about LSN;[4] Martin went on stage in D.C. with the president of El Salvador two days later; and Lightfair opened five days after that. Because Sensity had already thought through its category strategy, it was able to use the unfolding events as a rolling strike. By Lightfair, "we'd generated so much buzz our booth was packed all the time," Lee recalled. The main strike event was supposed to be a late-afternoon function at Lightfair, with an open bar to lure attendees. Lee had initially worried that not many people would show up. The room could hold 338, but she only set up 200 chairs. Instead, attendees packed the hall. Stragglers who couldn't crowd into the room stood outside the open doors trying to hear. Like the best pirates, Sensity improvised and ended up hijacking the whole week.

The outcome? Soon after the strike, stories about Sensity and LSN appeared in the *New York Times* and *San Jose Mercury News* and at least a half-dozen trade publications. The connection to El Salvador lit up Latin America media and exploded across Spanish-language social media. The coverage teed up Light Sensory Networks as a legitimate "thing." People in the lighting industry started using the term. And since Sensity was the company that defined LSN and the problems it could solve, the company set itself up as category king. In the fall of 2014, Cisco publicly recognized Sensity as "the pioneer of Light Sensory Networks" as the two companies signed a "strategic relationship." Less than a year after that, Sensity got $36 million in funding from Cisco, Acuity Brands, GE Ventures, and Simon Property Group. And the company still had only eighty employees. Sensity was like a band of eighteenth-century pirates staying one step ahead of the world's most powerful navies. And it started with that week-long strike.

Electrifying the Market

A great lightning strike is a category-defining event. It evangelizes a new problem or an old problem that can be solved in a new way. It tells the world that this company—the one initiating the strike—knows how to define the problem and knows how to solve it. It makes potential customers believe that the company has the solution, and makes would-be competitors panic and call emergency board meetings.

A strike is an event or coordinated series of events in a small window of time. It can take many forms. It might be a hijack of an existing conference—which was Sensity's plan. It can be tied to a product unveiling or new round of funding. It could be a manufactured industry summit for the sole purpose of the strike. That's what Macromedia did when Al was there in 2004. The company created the Macromedia Experience Forum, inviting a couple hundred guests to a Marriott in Anaheim, California, to explore "new approaches to delivering great digital experiences." Among the speakers were former vice president Al Gore and Joseph Pine, coauthor of *The Experience Economy*. The event helped establish Macromedia as the "Experience Matters" company in the minds of industry executives.

Apple has been perhaps the best lightning striker of the twenty-first century. Its fall product unveilings and summer Worldwide Developers Conference have become hotly anticipated annual events, so Apple then essentially hijacks its own event for strikes that establish a category-defining product such as the iPad or Apple Watch. Like a true lightning strike, the Apple announcements have always been a concentrated show of force, with all parts of the company plus partners and an ecosystem synched together. Hollywood has perfected the blockbuster movie strike. An event—the movie premiere—focuses the attention of the media and the Hollywood ecosystem as a rush of advertising works to pull in as big an audience as possible over opening weekend. The whole idea is to establish the movie as a blockbuster right away, so people continue to think of the movie as a blockbuster that they must see. In 2002, MINI USA set out to create a new category of car based on the MINI Cooper's characteristics: the smallest car on the road, yet powerful and fun. The company's strike included a twenty-two-city tour of MINI cars riding on top of SUVs—which both played off the MINI's size and the fact that fun stuff like bikes and kayaks go on top of your SUV. MINI's ad campaign touted fun "motoring" instead of workaday driving—a POV of different, not better.

Lightning strikes are not a new phenomenon. We should point out that one of the most effective strikes in technology history happened in April 1964, when IBM unveiled its System/360 line of mainframe computers. Before that date, computers—then the size of a room—were one-off hand-made machines running customized software. The data and programming on one model of computer was useless on another. There was no such thing as a line of compatible machines. System/360 created a new category in computing—a true system that could expand as a business grew. Though by 1964 IBM had been in existence for fifty years, the 360 was a bet-the-company endeavor. The full force of IBM shifted to the 360, and all the pieces, from engineering to marketing and sales, had to come together for the unveiling. On that day, IBM hosted several hundred reporters and customers at the main event in its Poughkeepsie, New York, factory. At the same time, IBM officials in 165 cities around the world put on parallel events. (No way to webcast an event in 1964!) The details of the announcement were purposely overwhelming in scope, designed to scare the hell out of competitors. The 360 included six models of different processor power, a range of options for memory, and fifty-four different peripherals that included magnetic storage devices, printers, and punch card readers. IBM CEO Thomas Watson Jr. told the Poughkeepsie crowd that this radical product was "the beginning of a new generation, not only of computers, but of their applications in business, science and government."[5] It was the kind of category-defining language you'd want to hear at a lightning strike.

The IBM event knocked the industry on its ass. More than a thousand orders came in during the first four weeks and another one thousand during the next four months. (Remember, this is for expensive giant machines that run a whole business, not some personal toy, so a thousand orders was unprecedented.) By the end of 1966, IBM had about 8,000 360s installed and was shipping 1,000 a month. IBM's revenue in 1966 would be $4.2 billion, about double that of just four years before. One-third of IBM's 190,000 employees in 1966 had been hired since the 360 program began. In 1964, IBM had seven significant competitors. By 1971, two were gone and the rest added together represented a blip in IBM's market share. The System/360 strike—the culmination of a masterful execution of category design—set up IBM to completely dominate the computer industry for the next twenty-five years.

What a Lightning Strike Does to Brains

In the second quarter of 2015, VCs invested $32.5 billion in 1,800 companies around the world.[6] That was just in one quarter. For every company that gets VC money, another 50 or 100 get started on angel investments or just maxing out the founders' credit cards. The cost of developing and launching a software-based product has fallen by a factor of 100 or more in the past twenty-five years, so vastly more products get developed and launched. All of this adds up to an incredible amount of noise. So many companies and so many products and services get unleashed on the public and compete for space in our brains. If a company can win a little slice of brain space, it succeeds. If it doesn't, it's finished. One way to get shelf space in the brain is to do something so big and audacious, it gets the target audience's attention and establishes a thought that goes like this: "That company understands my problem better than any other, and must have the solution."

That's the simple argument for a lightning strike. You've got to do something to cut through the noise and get into people's brains. It's true for enterprise-facing companies that need to reach business buyers, and it's true for consumer-facing companies that have to broadcast to the masses.

But there are also deep business reasons for burrowing into brains and establishing the idea that your company is creating and leading a new category. These reasons go back to research from the 1960s and 1970s. Ries and Trout cited it in *Positioning*. The authors noted that the leader is "the one who moves the ladder [that is, a category] into the mind with his or her brand nailed to the one and only rung."[7]

Another justification came up over happy hour drinks in Palo Alto with Richard Melmon, who cofounded Electronic Arts and is now a partner with Bullpen Capital. When Melmon looks at start-ups in the 2010s, he thinks back to the beginning of his career, when the technology industry embraced a study from Boston Consulting Group called the Experience Curve.[8] The study, based on data, showed that a market leader—essentially, a category king—gains knowledge and experience faster than runner-ups, so it quickly learns how to make better products at lower cost than competitors, and learns more about customers and the market than competitors, all of which can be used to solidify and expand a lead. BCG proved the power of category strategy fifty years ago. But, as Melmon said, the advantages of the Experience Curve begin with planting that leadership position into the brains of potential customers. "This is not just an idea—it's physics," Melmon told us. "Your brain has neurons and connections, and it's about physically implanting that thought in your brain, altering the actual physical structure."[9] If a company can do something to implant that thought in potential customers' brains, it lowers the amount of work that company has to do to acquire new customers. In other words, the cost and difficulty of acquiring customers goes down for the leader, while at the same time making it harder for competitors to alter that thought, which increases those competitors' cost and difficulty of acquiring new customers. The customer-acquisition advantage rolls up to other Experience Curve advantages, creating a flywheel that keeps empowering the category king while leaving competitors at a disadvantage.

A lightning strike is an efficient way to start altering brain patterns and establish the idea that your company is the category leader. A strike hits hard and fast. It is designed to burrow into the highest number of targeted brains as possible in as short a time as possible, immediately putting competitors on the wrong end of the Experience Curve. It worked for IBM in 1964, for Apple in the 2000s, and for companies like Sensity in the 2010s. Sometimes a great strike and its aftermath create such an overwhelming Experience Curve advantage, no one wants to fund the competition. If competing start-ups can't get funded by top-tier VCs, or if competing projects inside major corporations get canceled, challenges to the category king die before they even arise.

How to Aim Lightning

Actual lightning doesn't start out by choosing its target. It randomly seeks out some unfortunate soul who, for instance, happens to be the tallest thing on a wide-open beach. In business, though, a lightning strike has to work the other way around. You have to start by precisely identifying the target and the desired outcome, and work back from there.

Sensity's Light Sensory Network was half lighting and half networking and data. The company could have introduced its concept at an enterprise technology conference, where attendees would've instantly understood LSN. But category kings need to establish *different*, not just *better*. Technologists in the emerging era of the Internet of Things might not have seen LSN as all that different—networked lights might've come off as another IoT play that happened to be embedded in lights instead of thermostats or shoes. Sensity didn't aim to sell lights to technologists—it wanted to sell technology to lighting people. The company realized that a strike at Lightfair could be an industry-changing moment that would establish the problem LSN would solve in the brains of the people who design, build, and buy lighting. "Lightfair was all about lighting, and here we were talking about sensors and networks," CEO Martin said. "We thought, if we play this right, in twenty years this show will be about services and apps delivered over lightning networks, not just about lights."[10]

So as Sensity considered its target audience and desired outcome, it concluded it wanted to make lighting people start thinking that dumb lights were a problem—or at least a waste of resources—and that LSN was the most powerful, thought-through solution. Anyone considering a lightning strike needs to go through a similar thought process. A strike can't be expected to hit every possible audience all at once. Better to hit the right audience—including the right accounts, analysts, influencers, and press—at the right time to produce an outcome that sets the Experience Curve in motion.

The next question is when and where to strike so you reach the right audience. Some of this will be driven by the calendar. Remember, we recommend planning a strike for three to six months out, because a parallel purpose of a strike is to drive internal company mobilization. So pull out the calendar and see where your audience might be in three to six months. Trade shows and industry events can be target-rich environments. The more specific the show or event, the better chance you'll have of making noise and hijacking the conversation. Lightfair turned out to be perfect for Sensity. Some giant stampede of a convention like the Consumer Electronics Show would've been a disaster. Sensity would've gotten lost in the noise.

Trade shows and industry events aren't the only options. A company can create its own event, where it can invite its target audience of potential customers, industry analysts, and press. This is effective only if the event seems grander than a product announcement. Your target audience won't turn out for a glorified commercial, but they will turn out for good content, high-level networking—and an open bar. Sure, it can be expensive to put on an event like that, but it costs a lot less and can be more impactful than, for example, a national TV ad campaign.

Apple's tactic is to turn its major product releases into lightning strikes, especially when those products are meant to create a new category, as was the case with the iPod, iPhone, iPad, and Apple Watch. IBM's 360 was similarly both a product launch and strike. Not all product launches are lightning strikes and not all strikes have to include product launches. Consider your audience, the calendar, and your product schedule, and see what makes sense.

We've also seen strikes organized around a major funding event. When Google filed to go public, it used the release of its S-1 to announce it was going to be a new category of technology company. This is when Google laid out its "don't be evil" mantra. The founders' letter released with the S-1 began: "Google is not a conventional company. We do not intend to become one." It was pitching different, not better. It would focus on the long term and take crazy chances. It would be run by a triumvirate of Larry Page, Sergey Brin, and Eric Schmidt, not by a single CEO. There was no physical event involved in this strike. It was more of a communications and media event, led by the founders and aimed at the financial community and technology ecosystem.[11] Other companies have organized lightning strikes around private financings or other major financial milestones.

Once you identify the who, when, and where of a strike, the next question is: what's the content?

There are two requirements.

The first is that the content has to be big, bold, and different enough to cut through the noise and reach the brains of the target audience. That could mean engaging a superstar speaker like Bill Clinton or going onstage with the president of El Salvador. It could mean saying something no one has heard before (like a company saying it won't be evil). It could mean demonstrating a product that takes people's breath away (an iPhone). If there's any debate, lean toward playing bigger and bolder. Remember that this is *lightning*. You're not hedging your budget so you can spread marketing resources all over like peanut better. You're pumping everything you've got into this one bolt from the heavens.

The second requirement for content is that it has to evangelize the category problem first and your product or service second. Use the strike to identify the problem that can be solved, and then help your audience come to the same aha you had about how to solve it. Begin taking them on a from/to journey—from what they know now, to how things can be if they adopt your solution. If you lead with your solution and the audience doesn't yet understand the problem, whatever you say will bounce off their brains and land with a clunk on the floor. The problem is the key that unlocks your target audience's minds.

Don't forget that the event itself has to match the content and audience, or else the message will be lost. Writes Salesforce's Benioff, who has hosted numerous strike-like events: "The event is the message. Ensure that every decision you make—from venue to food to speakers—reflects well on your business and conveys your message." A classy health-care summit with Bill Clinton would feel off-kilter in a strobe-lit nightclub serving appletinis at the bar.

Once you know the when and where and what kind of lightning strike you're going to do, it's time to circle back to the previous chapter on mobilization to make sure the messages of the strike are grounded in reality—that products work, for instance, and the sales force is ready to roll. A successful lightning strike needs the equivalent of both an air war and a ground war. Air wars are about perception and changing people's minds. But that stalls if the ground troops aren't ready to come in behind the air cover and demonstrate working products and close deals.

We want to throw one other tactic into the mix. Sometimes it works well to tease—to let out a little bit of the message to prime the audience. Hollywood, again, is great at this. Consider the trailers for the 2015 *Star Wars* movie released half a year before the movie was due out, setting social media afire. Origami did something similar in July 2015, when it got a good deal of press attention for floating the idea of "marketing signals"—a hint at its upcoming lightning strike to introduce Marketing Signal Measurement. Apple's convenient "leaks" of product information do the same kind of audience-priming work. In our advisory practice, we call these teasing events thunderclaps.[12] A well-timed, intriguing thunderclap can help make the lightning strike effective.

To sum up, by the time you get to the day of your strike, you are ready to bring your new category to life. You would have identified and defined the category, developed a point of view, organized the company and strategy around that true north, and mobilized the company to be ready to storm the market. You'll have done a whole lot of heavy-lifting category design work to be ready for this day so that when you unleash the lightning strike on the world, it will improve your odds of becoming a category king. This is the work that helps you play bigger.

And now it's time to put on your pirate hat and play the role of cagey opportunist. Arrr!

Hijacks and Hijinks

One of our favorite pirate stories goes back to the earliest days of Salesforce.com. In December 2000, when the company was twenty months old and barely a blip on the tech industry radar, gigantic Microsoft, then the industry's superpower, announced it was buying Great Plains Software. If you looked at Great Plains through a prism in just the right way, the company could be seen as a Salesforce competitor. Salesforce CEO Benioff sent a memo to his staff poking fun at the deal and suggesting that the merger was only going to hasten the demise of software-based CRM in favor of cloud-based CRM. Benioff said in the memo that "Microsoft Great Plains will cause 'Great Pains' to the software CRM players who built their products in Microsoft's path.'" And then Benioff leaked the memo to business journalists, who couldn't resist using the "Great Pains" pun in their stories.[13] The tactic gave Salesforce a free ride on Microsoft's news—and associated the Salesforce brand with Microsoft. That's what we call a hijack. To increase the odds of becoming a category king, smart companies don't waste time and money on pointless vanilla, overly polite public relations. They go for PR that is opportunistic and edgy. And one good way for an upstart to leverage PR is to hijack some bigger company's PR or news.

A lightning strike is, really, a beginning—the opening salvo in defining, developing, and dominating a new category. Once the strike is over, a company has to relentlessly execute on its category strategy, over and over again, for years. While the initial strike can knock back potential competitors, you have to finish them off with blow after blow. And while a lightning strike is intended to lodge a new category into the brains of potential customers, you have to reinforce that idea with a constant drumbeat of messages.

Hijacks are a good way to do that.

Earlier in the book, we told Dave's story of Coverity hijacking news about software problems in the Toyota Prius, landing him on TV to talk about the value of testing software—which reinforced the category Coverity was creating. That was a classic hijack of a major ongoing news story. Sometimes it works to hijack your own news. Amazon.com hijacked its own 2002 IPO. Brad Stone wrote that "Bezos believed a public offering could be a global branding event that solidified Amazon in customers' minds"—not to mention that it could be used to beat down Barnes & Noble, which was then trying to wrestle the online book market away from Amazon.[14]

A cruel thing about lightning strikes is that you can't relax after pulling off that first one. You need to get busy with hijacks. And you need to start planning the next strike. In fact, we recommend three to six strikes to firmly establish a category, each within six months of the previous one. If you're a real pirate, you'll establish a rhythm of strikes and hijacks that constantly barrage customers and competitors with reminders about the category, the problem you've defined, and the solution you're offering. Once you burrow into people's brains, you want to deepen those grooves and make them permanent. This relentless pummeling is a job for the entire company, not just a few individuals in marketing. The follow-up strikes and hijacks can't just be *marketing* events; they have to be *company* events. The messages need substance behind them, so the company must mobilize continuously, building the muscles that back up the words. All in all, this becomes an ongoing exercise in total execution.

We learned this tactic of strikes and hijacks when Christopher and Dave helped pull off a potent pirate campaign in the software industry during their years at Mercury Interactive. Mercury's relentless execution across products and sales, coupled with nine total lightning strikes, took Mercury from a company hardly anyone heard of in 2002 to an acquisition by Hewlett-Packard in 2006 for $4.5 billion—admittedly with some ignoble bumps along the way.

Mercury was cofounded in 1989 by Amnon Landan, who as a young man hunted terrorists for the Israeli military, and entrepreneur Aryeh Finegold.[15] In its first years, the company was in the unglamorous business of software quality testing—the kind of stuff that goes on deep inside software development departments and stays invisible to everyone else. Mercury had become the software quality leader. As Christopher tells it, around 2000 Landan wanted to play bigger and become a top-five software company, and he hired Christopher and Dave to help. Mercury started building technology and making acquisitions so it could monitor and optimize software at every level throughout an enterprise. But as happened at Macromedia, Mercury's expanded product line was running the risk of becoming a bag of doorknobs—a gaggle of software products that didn't add up to a category. Mercury had to make its products make sense with each other, and tell a larger story about Mercury's offering if it was going to achieve its lofty goals. Mercury needed to define a new category, and then design and dominate it. That category turned out to be Business Technology Optimization, or BTO.

The POV that Mercury crafted about BTO was that your

business is running on software, and if the software is not performing well then the business is not performing well. If you want to optimize your business, Mercury said, you have to optimize your technology. Mercury's mantra became "Run IT like a business." It helped that the timing was right. In the early 2000s, the technology industry was still reeling from its dotcom crash hangover, and corporate customers wanted to drive down IT costs and optimize what they already had. Landan, CFO Doug Smith, and the others leading Mercury, with assistance from Christopher and Dave, crafted a point of view that captured the zeitgeist. Once it had a POV, the company needed a lightning strike to get attention.

The most important BTO strike happened in 2002 in New York, with the emotions from the 9/11 attacks on the World Trade Center still raw. The company created its own event, flying in 150 CIOs for a half-day agenda that included talks by Steve Forbes and Lou Dobbs, who then was CNN's popular business anchor. The day ended with a dinner on Ellis Island, where each guest got to see the registry that their ancestors signed when they arrived in the United States. That year, Mercury brought in about $400 million in revenue.

From there, as Christopher says, the company became a category execution machine. For the next four years, it kicked out a strike every six months—nine in all. In 2003, Landan announced his intention to make Mercury one of the top five software companies in the world, challenging the likes of Microsoft and SAP. The whirlwind of activity landed Landan on the cover of *Forbes* as its 2003 Entrepreneur of the Year. "We were hammering away at our competitors, our partners, our customers," Christopher recalls. "We wrapped everything in the context of BTO. It was BTO, BTO, BTO, all the time. We set the agenda, picking off topics important to IT. Every strike was a problem that we could solve with BTO. We'd explain their problem and put BTO out as the answer."

Mercury World, the company's conference, featured an Elton John concert one year. In between the strikes, Christopher and Dave's team pulled off hijacks. When Oracle bought PeopleSoft in 2004, Christopher borrowed from Benioff's playbook and got quoted saying the merger would be like watching two porcupines mating. When the concept of outsourcing software projects to India took off—amid controversy about sending jobs offshore—Mercury hijacked that shift, inserting itself as an expert on making offshoring work and then partnering with India's Wipro. "We'd figure out what was going on in the world, and then put ourselves in the center of it," Christopher says.

Now, as we said, there were some unfortunate parts of the Mercury story. In 2005, a number of tech companies—even Apple—ran afoul of the U.S. Securities and Exchange Commission over the way they accounted for stock options. Mercury got caught in that net. Landan and three other executives at Mercury (not Christopher or Dave) were fired by the board and investigated by the SEC. Mercury's stock price got cut in half by the markets and the chaos resulted in Mercury's delisting from NASDAQ. But here's the thing: As we said earlier, a category needs its king. It wants its king to succeed. Often, the category loves its king. When the financial scandals hit, Mercury's customers kept buying. The quarter when the worst news came out wound up being Mercury's best quarter ever. And in the end, because Mercury defined, developed, and dominated a significant new category called BTO, it was still valuable despite its difficulties. The company may have stumbled, but the category did not. The demand—the pull—for Mercury's products went on. In 2006, Mercury topped $1 billion in revenue. That year, HP agreed to buy Mercury for $4.5 billion.

Christopher's and Dave's experience at Mercury drove a lot of our ideas about lightning strikes and hijacks, and informed our belief that relentlessly executing on those tactics solidifies both the category and the position of the king. Since the start of this book, we have talked about how category kings design and develop a company, a product, and a category at the same time. That development starts with defining the category and continues through mobilization, lightning strikes, and hijacks until the category and king stand so solid they can't be brought down by a scandal, a strategic screwup, a competitor, a recession, or just about anything else.

If you get to that point, you are the category king of a vibrant, dynamic category. You have won. You are the envy of all those who have not won. And this is when you can use your position to become one of the rare breeds in global business: an enduring machine of continuous category creation.

The Play Bigger Guide to Strikes, Hijacks, and Attention Grabbing

Step One: Who?

The whole category design process must be driven by the CEO or whoever is the organization's supreme leader, and so the lightning strike, because of its role in category design, has to be conceived and supported by the leadership team. We recommended that the whole mobilization process be led by a strike master controller, who coordinates all the mobilization that has to come together on the day of the strike.

You also need someone who can pull off the strike itself—the actual event. The job is a combination of event planner and internal company wrangler. This person must have strong cross-functional skills, be detail oriented, love spreadsheets, and have the respect of the CEO. This is not a traditional role—you won't find a strike leader position on LinkedIn. It's just someone who can get shit done and is not afraid to be a pirate. Since events and news can be different around the world, a strike leader in a global organization might want to assemble a tight, coordinated team of people in different regions. Together this team must present a single source of truth for the entire organization for all deadlines, actions, and owners.

Another position to fill is the chief hijacker. This is probably your head of communications. It should be someone who is creative and opportunistic, understands the context around your company, can build good relationships with the media, and ideally is a pirate—someone who is willing to mix it up and take chances.

Step Two: Plan the Big Strike

This happens in parallel with the mobilization. As the whole company starts moving, the strike needs to be planned and executed. We recommend a kickoff meeting to set deadlines, set expectations for what will happen at the strike, and agree on the outcomes that are the goals of the strike. Ideally, the strike leader has a one-page master status report that lists all the dependencies and where they stand. This can be tricky because, as described earlier, a lot has to get done and it has to get done in the right order. The master status report is the truth. Set up a weekly meeting to go over the master status sheet with department heads. It will become obvious who's not delivering, and that will create natural pressure from teammates on those individuals.

Step Three: Plan the Event

While the whole company must mobilize behind the strike, the strike itself—the event and activities surrounding it—must be carefully planned and executed. Part of this job is event planning—getting the venue right, setting the tone, getting butts in seats, making sure everything runs smoothly. Make sure someone with those skills is on the team and in synch with the mobilization.

The event is part of the story, so make sure it all strikes the right note, addresses the right audience, and brings together all of the mobilization work in one place—the perception air wars coupled with the product and sales ground wars.

Step Four: Codify the Documents

While working on category design, you would have produced a boatload of material—the POV, blueprint, ecosystem and so on. Now that work has to be transferred into print and infused into everything the company presents. The POV must drive the website content and experience; the POV, taxonomy, and blueprint all go into sales presentations and training boot camps. Press releases must communicate the POV and content of the lightning strike. Every word counts. Not one word from the company should be out of synch with the category design work.

Step Five: Go Time

If everything has been planned and executed, even a last-minute news event or out-of-the-blue opportunity can be absorbed or hijacked, as Sensity showed. The day of the strike, you should feel confident that all will go smoothly, or even better than expected.

Immediately after, keep the execution machine going. Start selling. Turn on the marketing machine. Launch an ad campaign. Begin the pirate PR hijacks.

Step Six: Evaluate and Keep Going

The strike does not end after the event. Take a hard look at all of the results. Be honest. What worked? What didn't? Why? Learn, adjust, and keep executing. As Mike Tyson said, everybody has a plan until they get punched in the mouth. But then, alter the plan.

Look for signs of your strike's impact on competitors and pour gas on those fires. Look for the dent in the universe and keep pounding. Your exhausted teams might have that thousand-mile stare. Give them a breather, reward them with time and money, then get them back in the field and keep rolling.

And plan how to dominate and expand your category over time.

Part III

The Enduring
Category King

(Or, the Part About
How Pirates, Dreamers, and Innovators
Become Legendary and Dent
the Universe)

8

The Flywheel: From Category King to Legendary King

How to Become Legendary and Dent the Universe

Facebook started as a directory that would help college students hook up. A decade later, it was creating the global social graph.

Google started as a search engine, and fifteen years later was an intimate partner in the way billions of people operated their lives.

Amazon.com started selling books, and twenty years later was the world's most powerful online retailer.

Starbucks started by selling good coffee in a cozy café. Thirty years later it reigned as the world's "third place"—our sanctuary outside the home or office.

How did these companies get from this to that? The answer: They secured a position as a category king, then put a flywheel in motion that helped them continuously grow their category potential, all the while guided by a powerful point of view.

Simple, huh?

Physics of a Flywheel

Up to this point in the book, most of what we've written has been about defining and developing a category. This is the part about domination.

And we'll take it a step further. Once a category king dominates a category, it can use that position to expand the category,
taking the category potential to higher levels—in other words,
increasing the company's total addressable market, or TAM. The
handful of category kings that go on to become powerful forces
relentlessly expand their categories. And they do it in a way that
allows them to always be the king of the category they define.

Some category kings don't do this. VMware developed its virtualization category and then pretty much stopped, but the category
potential has proven to be so big and VMware is so dominant, the
company should be able to harvest the category for a long time.
There's nothing wrong with a good category-harvesting strategy—
which we'll come back to later.

Category expansion works when a king builds what we call—
with an homage to Jim Collins's *Good to Great*—a category flywheel. If a company executes on everything we've written thus far
in this book, it will naturally build and set in motion a flywheel,
and that flywheel will return the favor by constantly reinforcing
the category king position and giving the company the strength,
resources, and permission to push outward and expand the category potential.

World-class category kings get massively rewarded for their
category-expanding strategies—or, rather, for embedding this kind
of strategy into the DNA of the company culture. Facebook in 2015
had averaged almost $20 billion a year in new market cap created
since its founding. That's more than the value of one Workday, every
year. Many people believe the key driver of success for a company
like Facebook is great execution with product and sales. While that's
critical, it's not the whole story. Facebook has continually expanded
the category potential of social networking while simultaneously
conditioning its investors so they understand the strategy. Investors
buy into not just Facebook's execution, but the total future potential
of the category, with Facebook as its king.

We'll start here by describing flywheels and how they work, and then tell you some real-life stories—because these are the stories behind the ascension of great companies like Facebook, Google, Amazon.com, Starbucks, and others. This draws on material from previous chapters, but don't think we're handing you a beer with just backwash left in the bottle. This is how everything we've described comes together in the most legendary category kings.

The foundation of a flywheel is made up of the three elements we described early in the book: company design, product design, and category design. If all three are strong and working in synch, they reinforce one another and create a compounding effect on both the company and market. Since a good category king designs all three at the same time, it designs a category that's a perfect fit for the products it offers and the kind of company it operates— giving the king a natural and unshakable advantage.

A company's value is rooted in its category. First comes category potential. Investors need to believe that a company is in a category with great untapped potential, and if so, the investors will pay for access to that category. Next is the company's position within that category. The category king, as we've said, will eat up the majority of a category's economics, so investors want to put their money in the king. Finally, there's performance or execution. These are results—maybe sales or user growth—that show that a company is effectively delivering products or services that the category desires. When category potential, position in the category, and execution all come together in investors' minds, they see the future and want a piece of it.

If you think about Google and Facebook in the 2010s, the company, product, and category are indistinguishable from one another. Search is Google and social networking is Facebook. The more people think a company is a category king, the more people's brains are made happy buying and using products from the king. Users would expect any other company or product entering those categories to act and look like Google or Facebook, but nobody can act and look like Google or Facebook as well as Google and Facebook. The argument is kind of tautological, but that's the point—the actions and benefits of company design, product design, and category design working together circle back on themselves. The only thing that can break the cycle is the introduction of an entirely different category that pulls customers away from the old one. Microsoft's search engine Bing could never beat Google because it tried to be *like* Google. (And the more Microsoft compared Bing to Google, the more it reinforced Google's leadership position in people's brains.) The only way Google will be weakened is if a new category of search emerges that makes the old category seem outmoded.

To keep the flywheel spinning true and not flying off its axis, a king needs a strong POV. The POV gives the company a genetic, ingrained understanding of where it's going. The POV has to be tailored so that the ambitions of the company fit with its capabilities; otherwise the company won't be able to execute and its disappointing performance will scare off investors. But the POV has to show the way forward so the company, product, and category can expand together, increasing category potential without making the flywheel tilt off balance and crash.

A constant beat of mobilizations and lightning strikes acts as the force that throws the flywheel into a stronger and more unrelenting, compounding spin. Each strike and everything it entails gives the flywheel another shove. This constant commitment to play bigger has the added bonus of helping to keep gravity in check. The realities of day-to-day business and life always pull against category design. The perpetual motion of the flywheel acts as a counter, drawing focus and effort back to category design.

The flywheel carries with it a whole package of tangible, commercial advantages. The Experience Curve that we discussed earlier kicks in, and that allows the category king to do more with less than any of its competitors. As the flywheel spins, it opens a deeper chasm between the king and its followers, making it very difficult for the king to be dethroned. Once the flywheel is whirring, if some challenger tries to stick a finger in it, it's going to lose a finger.

A category king builds an ecosystem, and the ecosystem in turn adds momentum to the flywheel. In the Google and Facebook flywheel, users are a material part of the ecosystem. Every time users do anything on Google or its sister services, they contribute to Google's database of knowledge and that fine-tunes results from its algorithms, so Google gets better faster than any entity with fewer users. On Facebook, users add content and connect to each other, contributing constantly to Facebook's flywheel. Outside developers are a critical element of most technology ecosystems, and they have a huge impact on the flywheel. They build add-ons and plug-ins and tangential products that extend far beyond any one company's reach. Peripheral makers have the same effect—some of GoPro's strength as a category king comes from all the doohickey attachments made by other companies. As a king solidifies its position, developers move their allegiance from competitors to the king, creating a virtuous cycle that lures even more developers. Anyone who touches a king's product is part of its ecosystem and will feel the weighty pull into the king's flywheel.

Money helps fuel the flywheel's energy. The stronger the flywheel's spin, the more money it attracts. The king has money or valuable equity to spend on acquisitions that distance it from competitors or expand the category. It has money to spend on advertising and marketing to reach a greater audience and overwhelm its competitors. The king gains pricing power, so it has more money to invest in products, sales, customer support systems, internal management systems—all of which add to the domination over competitors.

Data is an increasingly important element, especially for

cloud-based services, where every action by customers or anyone in the ecosystem gets captured and can be analyzed to improve products and serve customers better. Data will increasingly play a role in industries that didn't used to involve data—like cars, lights, homes, and restaurants.

And, of course, talent fuels the flywheel. The best people want to work for a king. They know when a company is going to change the way we do things, create new career opportunities, and compensate them well. As the king soaks up the best talent, that talent builds a more powerful company, product, and category. Recruiting against a category king is frustrating. Other companies in the space wind up with next-tier talent—or they move to Portland.

Round and round the flywheel goes, until its momentum becomes almost impossible to stop. When a flywheel spins fast enough, even a strategic blunder can't interrupt it. That's why Mercury could be investigated by the federal government and have its best sales quarter at the same time.

A flywheel can be the most powerful force in business. Get it started by employing category design. Guide it with a POV. Power it with lightning strikes and mobilizations. Grow it by expanding the category potential. Do all of that, and a company will increase its odds of becoming not just a category king, but a *legendary* category king that alters everyday life and work.

Category King Stories Through the Flywheel Lens

"When you get started as a college student you limit your scope," Facebook CEO Mark Zuckerberg told *Vanity Fair* in the summer of 2015. "It's like, 'I'm going to build this thing for the community around me.' Then it's 'I'm going to build this service for people on the Internet.' But at some point you get to a scale where you decide we can actually solve these bigger problems that will shape the world over the next decade."[1]

If you pull back from the story of Facebook, you can see how a relentlessly accelerating flywheel, guided by Zuckerberg's strong and prescient POV, step by step expanded the potential market for the category of social networking that Facebook defined. Only the most brilliant category designers get to that kind of nirvana.

Facebook—back when it was called TheFacebook—started in the early 2000s on the Harvard campus, and users could register only if they had a harvard.edu email address. Its first expansion of category potential was when it opened up to other college campuses. Social networks such as sixdegrees and Friendster were already cropping up, but Zuckerberg essentially defined his category as social networking for college students. The category, as Zuckerberg alluded to in his *Vanity Fair* comment, matched the capabilities of the company at the time, and vice versa. Or, to use a metaphor we called on earlier, the suit fit. The campus-first strategy also proved to be key to getting a flywheel going. Co-founder Dustin Moskovitz even studied the effect of choosing that category, and concluded that the density of social relationships on college campuses was important to the site quickly getting momentum. Each time Facebook opened up to a new campus, the flywheel got an extra push. Once the site penetrated a large number of colleges, Facebook gave its flywheel a huge push by expanding to high schools—expanding the category potential from "college students" to "students." By October 2005, Facebook had about 5 million users, nearly all of them students.[2] Facebook was playing bigger, step by step.

Behind the scenes of this disciplined approach of defining a category that fit the company, Zuckerberg developed a POV that reached far beyond his start-up's position. Facebook's pushes on its flywheel and its category expansions were sometimes planned and sometimes serendipitous, yet always guided by Zuckerberg's evolving POV about connecting people online with their real-world relationships. In 2005, as more people started carrying cell phones armed with cameras, Facebook added the ability to post photos. The enthusiasm from users took Facebook by surprise. Within six weeks, photos had consumed all the storage Facebook planned to use for the next six months. Facebook was still a student site, but the response to the photo application led Zuckerberg to the idea of the social graph—that Facebook would map the connections between everyone on earth. "He was formulating a broader and broader theory about what Facebook really was," Sean Parker told author David Kirkpatrick for *The Facebook Effect*.[3]

By 2006, Facebook's flywheel was picking up serious speed. Money came in from top VCs—Jim Breyer, Peter Thiel, Marc Andreessen—and from a significant deal with Microsoft. The money fed the flywheel and opened a gap with competitors. In 2005 and 2006, the mainstream press churned out Facebook stories. The site added its Newsfeed, giving users a running report on what their friends were doing. In 2007, Facebook cultivated an ecosystem, opening up Facebook to developers and organizing its first developers conference, F8. By the end of the year, Facebook had lured 250,000 developers and 24 million users. The compounding flywheel became powerful enough to pull Facebook through a horrendous strategic decision. In November 2007, it introduced Beacon, which would automatically show all your friends what you just purchased on a partner site. The swift backlash about that invasion of privacy threatened to derail Facebook's category potential. (If people felt they couldn't trust Facebook, a lot fewer would choose to use it.) But the company's flywheel had enough momentum to carry the company through. Zuckerberg apologized for the mistake and killed Beacon.

By early 2008, Facebook's pace of growth picked up again. In the 2010s, Facebook stormed its way into mobile phones, designing the product for smartphones and buying messaging service WhatsApp. Since phones will reach perhaps billions more people than laptops, the moves expanded Facebook's category potential yet again. Over and over, Facebook has played bigger, redesigning its category, product, and company in synch with one another to expand its category potential. It kept building a sense that Facebook's domination was inevitable. A company's value is based on its category potential, its position in the category, and its execution. Facebook blew out its category potential to include everyone on earth, built a powerful flywheel that ensured its category king position, and has shown results that indicate it is executing on its promise. And that's why Facebook in the 2010s became the most valuable technology company founded in the twenty-first century.

This same lens helps us understand how other companies made themselves into global giants that changed life for hundreds of millions of people.

Google started as a simple search engine. It soon understood that search was a way to deliver useful information to people, so Page and Brin redefined the company's POV to say it was "organizing the world's information." That in turn expanded Google's category potential—the more kinds of information Google could organize beyond just what was on Web pages, the more users it could address. So Google digitized books, built out Google Maps, introduced Gmail, bought Picassa for photos, and bought You-Tube for video, each time bringing into the mix a new kind of information the company could organize. As it became clear that mobile phones would explode Google's category potential, Google developed Android to plant itself in that realm. All the while, Google built its flywheel—money, users, ecosystem, some of the smartest employees in the world, and more and more data—and cemented its place as king of whatever expanded category it defined. To top it off, Google executed, showing results that proved it could keep its promises. Put it all together, and Google emerged as a legendary category king.

Point the lens at Amazon.com. It started with books, which was a category with limited potential, but the category fit the company and the product the company could build at the time. As the company conquered the books category, it looked for a likely category expansion—which turned out to be digital media such as CDs and DVDs. It built its flywheel, giving Amazon the power and permission to keep expanding its category until the category reached into nearly every corner of retail. The flywheel even helped Amazon do something extremely rare: define, develop, and dominate an entirely new category outside of its original mission. That new category was cloud services, and Amazon Web Services is the category's king. (More on that in the next chapter.) So Amazon expanded its category potential to include almost every online shopper in North America, Europe, and most of Asia; it nailed its position as king in most of those regions (though not all); and it continues to prove its execution through its results. In mid-2015, Amazon's market cap was greater than that of the previous monster force in retail, Wal-Mart.

Every kind of legendary category king—not just those in technology—builds a flywheel and continuously expands its category potential. Starbucks is a great example. Howard Schultz bought a Seattle coffee shop, but like Zuckerberg he had in his head a much grander POV: that Starbucks would be the world's home away from home. The category potential was enormous, and Schultz did a brilliant job designing and developing his "third place" category at the same time as he designed his company and product to fit it. He kept the flywheel spinning, ensuring Starbucks was always its category's king, and except for a hiccup after the 2008 financial meltdown, Starbucks executed on its promises. By 2015, the company was worth $80 billion and the brand was among the most recognizable in the world.

The flywheel and category potential also give us a glimpse into why some legendary category kings sputter. It's worthwhile to look back at history, because, as philosopher George Santayana wrote, "Those who cannot remember the past are condemned to repeat it." Microsoft in its glory days had a reputation as a copier and fast follower—in fact, a lot of industry watchers believed that tendency was a Microsoft strength. But through our lens, the story looks different.[4]

When in 1981 IBM decided to use Microsoft's MS-DOS in the first IBM PCs, Microsoft essentially won the lottery. But Gates quickly recognized the completely new category he was creating: PC operating systems. He designed that category in parallel with his product and company, and the success of the IBM PC and its clones helped Microsoft build its flywheel. But that category potential of PC operating systems was limited by the difficulty of using DOS and applications that ran on it. To expand its category potential, Microsoft had to make computers easier. It saw what Apple and Xerox were doing with graphics-based navigation and understood how it improved ease of use, so Microsoft developed Windows. Windows opened up the PC market to a wider audience, which allowed Microsoft to define a new category of ubiquitous personal computing, described in its famous POV: "A computer on every desk and in every home."[5] Every subsequent Microsoft move—Office, Outlook, Explorer—was a way to expand its category potential by either getting more computers on desks or into homes, or getting a bigger part of the software market for each of those computers. And in each case, Microsoft used its category king position on PCs to gain a monopoly position for everything it owned.[6] The Microsoft flywheel spun. Competitors couldn't compete. Through the 1990s, Microsoft reigned as the legendary category king of personal computer software.

And then? The category potential lost steam. In the 2000s, as cloud computing and mobile phones entered the mainstream, most people who wanted a computer had a computer, and people who had computers wanted to own less software because they could do most things on the Internet, on mobile apps or in the cloud. We also suspect that Microsoft was trapped by the gravitational pull of the profits from products like Windows, Office, and Exchange. As the company searched for new category potential, Microsoft tried things where it had no flywheel—in fact, it tried things where someone else already had a strong flywheel, which is almost always a losing proposition. The company followed Apple's category-defining iPod by trying to introduce Zune. It followed two mobile OS category kings—Google's Android and Apple's iOS—with phone operating systems that couldn't compete. It followed category king Google with Bing. It followed Apple's stores by opening Microsoft stores. All failed to get traction. For a decade, Microsoft's stock was stuck in neutral because its equation was broken: it was not creating new category potential, it could not usurp the king of the categories it was entering, and ultimately it wasn't executing on the areas outside its flywheel of computer software. Microsoft wasted a lot of money playing smaller.

The way for Microsoft to get its old mojo back will be for it to design a new category with new potential, and dominate the new category as a king. To do that, Microsoft would have to go right back to the beginning of this book and deploy category design.

The Tao of Category Potential

The Microsoft story brings us around to something we often say: there comes a time when every CEO of a category king realizes that her current position is the biggest inhibitor to growth. That moment arrives when she figures out that the category she dominates will soon run out of potential.

It's awesome to be a king. We just wrote most of this book about how to get to such a place of awesomeness. Your reward for winning: you get to do it all over again! No category king reigns over a category with unlimited potential. Even redwood trees don't grow to the moon. All category kings start out by designing and building a category they can handle—which is to say a category with distinct borders. So every king will get to the day when most of the addressable market has been, well, addressed. At that point it won't matter how well the company performs—the stock will not move up in a meaningful way until investors see more potential. To continue to grow with alacrity, the category king then has to design and build a new category with greater category potential. Companies such as Facebook or Amazon go through this cycle many times.[7]

In mid-2015, a company called ServiceNow wrestled with this situation, and discussed it with us.[8] Fred Luddy founded ServiceNow in 2003 and aimed it at a category of IT service management. The company offered a cloud-based way for IT departments to automate the way they track reported problems and solve them. This let IT departments serve their companies more effectively, and gathered data that could help companies optimize their technology. ServiceNow became the category king by the late 2000s. The company went public in 2012 at about a $2 billion market cap while its annual revenue was $93 million—so it was valued at 20 times revenue, a huge valuation. Why so high? Because ServiceNow had tapped a category with a lot of potential, made itself king, and delivered on its promises.

But ServiceNow inevitably was going to run into a problem: the number of IT departments that were its addressable market was limited to a few thousand, with a total potential user base of maybe 4 million to 8 million people. ServiceNow didn't already have all of them as customers, but investors could see that the potential market had borders, so the stock price stopped rising so quickly. In the value equation, ServiceNow had already gotten paid for the category potential of IT service management. The company was the clear category king, and it delivered results, but the stock had stalled. To get it moving again, the company needed to come up with greater category potential.

In early 2015, CEO Frank Slootman (who took over from Luddy) told *Fortune*: "Our mission is to basically drop the 'IT' from service management discussions. Instead of having people talking about IT service management, we just want them talking about service management, the implication being that it's an enterprise discipline."[9] What's going on here? ServiceNow had helped IT departments better service the other departments within a company. Now it wanted to use its technology—and tap the power of its flywheel—to help every department in a company service every other department. If it can automate and optimize the way human resources or marketing interacts with the rest of the company, it could massively multiply its potential base of customers and users—in other words, blow out its category potential. Most category kings don't look for new potential until they are in trouble. Success is a shitty teacher. But Slootman, his CMO Beth White, and others on the executive team got aggressive about creating new potential *before* there was a problem with the old potential. We'll be watching to see what happens with the ServiceNow story.[10]

How does a CEO know when it's time to expand the company's category potential? Some CEOs, like Zuckerberg and Bezos, seem to intuitively feel it. They come preloaded with a grand ambition—connect everyone! sell everything!—and see each category expansion as a step toward their dream.

For other leaders, company value can indicate a need for category expansion. If a start-up raises one round of financing but then can't gin up much interest in the next round, then one or more parts of its category strategy are broken. Same is true if a public company's stock price seems stuck in low gear for an extended time. Then it's time to expand category potential. Some executive teams of publicly traded, hypergrowth companies fall into a predictable trap when their growth slows as a result of bumping into the borders of their current category: rather than focusing on expansion, they think they can stimulate the stock price by improving profits. Without the category lens on their business, they get hoodwinked into thinking their investors want profits over growth. While all investors like profits, what drives the market cap of category kings is potential. More than one tech CFO has been left wondering why the company's value is shrinking as profits increase.

Another sign of stuck category potential is when you look up and realize you can count your potential customers. That happened to Dave at Coverity. There was a narrow number of possible buyers of Coverity's software testing products. It made for a nice business for Coverity, but not a business that was going to grow much. The category was too limited.

Then what should a CEO with a stuck category potential do? Well, she may get lucky and stumble onto the next category. The more disciplined approach—the way to increase odds of success—would be to go back and start the category design process all over again. This is why category design is emerging as a strategic discipline. It is a way to make sure all parts of the value equation make sense while expanding category potential in a way that excites investors, users, employees, and everyone in the ecosystem.

With that, we have a word of warning. We have seen—up close and way too personal—that one of the more dangerous things to do in business is to clearly identify a hot new category and then fail to become its king. A category is a problem to be solved in a new way, and once the public sees that problem, they can't unsee it. There is no way to unring a bell. The market will demand a solution. If you define that category and disappoint the market for any reason—you don't have the resources or wherewithal or whatever to become its king—then the market will look for a different king. This is why the old saw about "first-mover advantage" is mostly bullshit. The first mover has an advantage only if the first mover has the wherewithal to become king and deliver on its promises. Otherwise, the first mover goes kersplat. Think Webvan in grocery delivery, or MySpace in social networks, or all the early MP3 players before the iPod. Slack took flight in 2015 by occupying a category of business social networking that several companies had identified but didn't quite build and dominate.[11] We call category design a discipline for a reason. It's a serious weapon, not a toy. Use it unwisely and you can shoot yourself in the face.

Of Category Harvesting and Succession Planning

There is another scenario—the VMware scenario. It goes like this: Company defines a new category. Category potential quickly ramps up to monstrous. Demand explodes. The leadership designs a company that can reign as king, and the company builds a product that delivers on the category's promise. Stunning growth ensues. Value goes through the roof. In other words, the company has done everything right to become the king of a category with tons of potential for years going forward.

The company then decides it has won and will feast on the spoils. It doesn't expand the category or show any intent to do so. It doesn't *need* to—the category will be that rich for years to come. In other words, the company has itself a cash cow. And if the cow is breathtakingly abundant, the company doesn't need another one for a while—it just needs to milk this one for all it's worth. You might call this strategy cow milking,[12] but we'll go with a less pithy but probably more respectful term: category harvesting.

Category harvesting is a very different thing from category design. That's not to say it's bad. Harvesting is one of the most valuable skills in business, and the right thing to do when a king taps into giant category potential. Larry Bossidy and Ram Charan's classic book, *Execution: The Discipline of Getting Things Done*, is essentially a field guide to category harvesting. Many mature companies are in the business of harvesting their categories. Chrysler has been harvesting the minivan category since the 1980s.

Category harvesting requires a different mindset compared to category design. It's more about evolutionary improvement, tending the flywheel so it keeps its speed up, a lot of marketing and sales activity, and a focus on getting the highest profit margins possible. Great category designers almost always make for lousy harvesters—and vice versa.

The point here: If you're a founder or CEO who has gone through category design and made your company a king, you have a couple of directions to choose from. One is to define, develop, and dominate an even larger category, à la Facebook or Amazon. The other way to go is to stop category design and turn instead to harvesting. It's paramount to choose one clear direction or the other. Ambiguity around this destroys value.

How do you know from the outside if a company has made that switch? One leading indicator is that the leadership changes. Often, a category-design-oriented CEO gets bored with harvesting and leaves—or a category-design-oriented CEO tries to do harvesting and is bad at it, so she gets pushed out by the board. Almost every time a great category designer CEO leaves, you can bet that the succeeding CEO is a harvester.

Bill Gates was a category designer. Steve Ballmer probably was a great category harvester, except he was a harvester who tried to be a designer and fucked that up time and again. Gates handed Microsoft to his good friend Ballmer in 2000. The year before, Microsoft was the most valuable company ever. Ballmer couldn't bring Microsoft much new category potential, even though the company remained super-profitable as it harvested the shit out of Windows and Office. The stock dropped during the dot-com crash in 2000 and bumped along at those lower levels until the new CEO came along.[13] Microsoft shows how investors value top-line sales growth in expanding categories versus bottom-line profit growth in mature categories.

Diane Green at VMware was a category designer. The board pushed her out in 2008 and hired Paul Maritz as her successor. Maritz had been at Microsoft for fourteen years during the Windows superpower era, when he learned to be a great harvester.

At Intel, legendary category designer Andy Grove stepped down in 1998. He handed the CEO job to his good friend the Intel veteran Craig Barrett. Intel was a speeding locomotive. Barrett saw his job as keeping Grove's company on the tracks. Which he did. But then technology changed, moving to the Internet and mobility, and because Intel stayed on that same track, it lost its chance to lead in a new age. From 1998 to 2000, Barrett's first two years, Intel's stock soared. But those were the dot-com boom years. Almost all tech stocks soared. Just after 2000, Intel stock crashed back to earth. While harvesting its chip business to the hilt and making good profits, Intel did not develop great new category potential, so its equation broke.

Larry Ellison at Oracle was a legendary category designer. He remained at the top of his company, but hired a series of fantastic harvesters—particularly Safra Catz and Mark Hurd—to run things. Oracle has made all kinds of money over the years, but hasn't designed a new category.

Steve Jobs was, we believe, the best category designer of them all. What to make of Tim Cook in this regard? As of this writing, the jury is still out. However, in the mid-2010s there is an aspect of the Tim Cook story to watch for—and it will say a lot about the direction Apple takes in years to come. To show what we mean, let's turn back to IBM and the succession situation that led to the System/360 triumph.

From 1914 to 1956, IBM was built by Thomas Watson Sr. and became the world's first great computing company. He was the category designer of the category of data processing. But Watson Sr.'s era of computing was based on electromechanical technology. Computing was not digital. Data was stored on punch cards and calculations were done through a series of electric mechanisms. In the mid-1950s, as an aging Watson Sr. started backing away from his company, a new era of computing was being born, based on vacuum tubes, transistors, magnetic storage, and digital calculations. This new technology was called electronics.

Just as electronics emerged, Watson named his successor: his son, Thomas Watson Jr. The fact that the son of the powerful company builder took over just as technology changed turned out to be fortuitous for IBM. Watson Jr. wasn't just a son—he was a rebellious son. He didn't want to continue his father's legacy—he wanted to tear up his father's IBM and make it his own. Here is an image that captures the jarring transformation, from Kevin's biography of Watson Sr., *The Maverick and His Machine*. The description is what Watson Sr. saw when leaving IBM on his last day of work there: "On [Watson Jr.'s] orders, workers had ripped up the oriental rugs and dark wood that had been in the lobby since the 1930s, and installed a modern decor that included bright white floors, crimson walls, metallic desks, and a sleek, simple '702' on the wall above the computer housing." The son didn't even wait for his father to get out of the building.[14]

That shift to electronic technology gave the younger Watson the opportunity to take IBM through category design all over again, guided by his POV instead of his father's. Watson Jr. embraced electronic computing and wanted IBM to be its king. His stature as the son of the company builder gave Watson Jr. the power and permission to pull off this transformation. The new category-building effort began in earnest in the late 1950s. (Watson Sr. died in 1956, so old loyalists had no one to cling to.) By the early 1960s, the entire company was wrapped up in the grand System/360 drive, which has gone down in history as a bet-the-company program. IBM had given up harvesting its old business, and was completely focused on creating its new business. If the new business failed, the company would've been sunk.

System/360 was a spectacular success and remade IBM, at age fifty, into a category king with gigantic new category potential. From 1956, when the younger Watson took over, to 1971, when he retired, IBM quadrupled its number of employees and increased revenue by more than nine times. In Watson Jr.'s final year as CEO, IBM was the hottest stock in the world, worth the combined value of 21 of the 30 stocks that made up the Dow Jones Industrial Average.

But then, after Watson Jr., successive IBM CEOs were harvesters. They had a legendary category to tap, so that turned into big profits for a couple of decades. But even the greatest categories eventually run low, and that became IBM's dilemma in the 1990s. Its category was tired, and the company badly needed new category potential. Incoming CEO Louis Gerstner ended up finding it in the computing services and consulting business. In the 2010s, IBM again badly needs new category potential, which is why it began investing a billion dollars in developing its Watson cognitive computing platform.

So how about Apple and Tim Cook? Is Cook a Watson Jr., or is he a Ballmer or Barrett? Well, on the day of Apple's big Watch announcement in 2014, Cook talked to ABC News about Jobs: "There's not a day that goes by that I don't think of him. This morning, being here, I especially thought about him, and I think he would be incredibly proud to see the company that he left us."[15] Cook even tried to imitate Jobs's way of introducing new products onstage. But if Cook reveres Jobs too much, he can't be a Watson Jr., wresting Apple from its present to design and dominate a new category that opens up new category potential. Maybe the Apple of 2015 shouldn't do that yet—it has such stunning categories to harvest. You can bet we'll be watching Apple through this lens:

will Cook turn out to be a great category designer, a great harvester . . . or neither?

For CEOs of category kings, this issue becomes central to succession plans. Do you leave things to a category harvester, who will hone what you created and turn it into profits? Or do you leave things to a category designer, who will change what you created and turn it into category potential?

It's probably the most important decision a departing architect of a category king can make.

The Play Bigger Guide to Flywheels and Category Potential

Step One: Who?

The CEO or founder—the category designer in chief—is where this buck stops. The flywheel involves every aspect of the company and ecosystem, and only the CEO has the sight lines and influence to put all those pieces together. Similarly, only the CEO or equivalent leader can drive an expansion of category potential.

Step Two: Recommit to Category Design

If you've succeeded at category design and made yourself category king, the flywheel will take care of itself. If you're running out of category potential and need to expand it in a meaningful way, then it's time for your company to go back to the start of this book and go through category design once again.

Step Three: Figure Out Whether You're Done

If you're a category designer and you've built a king, you have a decision to make. You can either re-up on category design, or you can harvest the current category potential for all it's worth. If you're going to do the latter, you probably need to find a successor who is a great harvester. Or you can sell the company to a bigger company, which will then do the harvesting.

Step Four: The Double-Secret Other Choice

Oh, there is one other way this can all turn out, but it's highly unusual. This would be the path to creating a rare continuous category creation machine. It's hard to even find them in the wild. But we know of a few we can tell you about. Read on . . .

9

The Corporate Chapter: The Rare Art of Continuous Category Creation

How to Build to Last, Continue Crossing Chasms, and Avoid Innovator's Dilemma

Every legendary start-up wants to become a big old company.

That's the point, right? Some start-up founders are just looking for a way to sell out to Google so they can buy a boat and screw around for the rest of their lives. More power to 'em, but they're probably not the ones reading this book.[1] The kinds of founders who engage in category design, build a category king, fight gravity, and expand their category potential—the real pirates, dreamers, and innovators—want to build something that lasts for generations. Jobs, Bezos, Benioff, Page, Zuckerberg, Musk, and others like them would like nothing better than to know that someone who isn't yet born will run their company long after they are gone.

At the same time, many big old corporations are what legendary start-ups *don't* want to become. Big old corporations get their asses kicked by start-ups. Big old corporations have a reputation for playing it safe, changing slowly, and milking their cash cows dry rather than creating new categories. In fact, big old corporations are manifestly terrible at creating anything new. When Nielsen analyzed 20,000 products—mostly from big old corporations—introduced in the United States from 2008 to 2014, it found that just 74, or less than half a percent, actually broke through with sustained success.[2] So the odds of a start-up becoming a billion-dollar category king are better than the odds of a new product from a big old corporation creating a new category and succeeding over the long term. Yikes.

But there's another possible outcome. Some great, enduring companies build a culture of continuous category creation. In fact, they build a category creation machine that turns the big company's size and longevity—often seen as weaknesses—into an advantage.

Now, we greatly respect the long history of important research and writing on the subject of spurring innovation inside corporations. Peter Drucker was the master, writing that innovation for a corporation is not about inspiration but is instead a process of methodically analyzing opportunities.[3] Clayton Christensen's classic, *The Innovator's Dilemma*, describes why big companies have a hard time reacting to start-ups (it's basically the phenomenon of gravity that we wrote about earlier) and suggests that big companies should set up semi-independent skunk works that can more easily innovate. Geoffrey Moore's body of work addresses not just innovation and how to push innovation to a broad market, but also how to reinvent an ongoing company.[4] Jim Collins told us about the critical role of monster-innovation BHAGs (Big Hairy Audacious Goals) at enduring companies in *Built to Last*.[5] All of them are right. These people are giants, and we don't intend to be David showing up with a slingshot and a rock.

But we are showing up with a slightly different point of view. When we aim our lens at the companies that Drucker, Christensen, Moore, and Collins might admire, we often see category design at work. We believe that the same discipline that improves the odds of a start-up becoming a category king can improve the odds of a corporation renewing itself by creating, developing, and ultimately dominating new categories.

And What Will You Be Doing When You're 165 Years Old?

We'd like to tell you about a company you might think doesn't belong in this book. Corning, the glass company, seems like the antithesis of Silicon Valley. Founded in 1851, its headquarters is in the town of Corning, which is in the Finger Lakes region of western New York State and not near anything that might be called a city. Employees stay aboard at Corning for decades. The company's main business is making a substance that's been around almost as long as dirt. Its first big break came when Thomas Edison contracted with the company to make the glass for his invention called the lightbulb.

Corning, though, is a category creation machine. The company is still alive and vibrant because, over and over again in its history, it has defined, developed, and dominated important new categories of glass. It created and dominated the category of the television tube (the bulbous glass thing that made old-style TVs work), and the categories of laboratory glass (Pyrex, which can withstand high temperatures), catalytic converters (ceramics that scrub pollutants from car exhaust) and fiber optics (you know what those are), not to mention CorningWare, the hard-to-break dishes your mother probably had in her kitchen (Corning since sold that business). If you have a flat-screen TV from any manufacturer in the world, the glass is probably made by Corning, the king of that business. And if you pull out your smartphone, the super-hard touch-sensitive glass on the surface is almost certainly made by Corning, which is the category king with its brand known as Gorilla Glass.

We talked with CEO Wendell Weeks about the Gorilla Glass story, which shows how category creation works inside Corning—and how it can work inside any big entity. The story's catalyst is Steve Jobs, but its beginning goes back to the 1960s.[6]

One advantage big corporations have over start-ups is the ability to fund serious research and development, and Corning has long operated a research lab. Earlier in the book, we pointed out the two different kinds of insights that lead to category creation. One is a technology insight, which is the invention of a new technology that needs to find a market; the other is a market insight, which identifies a new opportunity that could be met by building a new technology. Most Silicon Valley start-ups begin with a market insight. A corporate research lab really has one singular purpose: to come up with technology insights.

At Corning, the lab is driven by what Weeks calls "grand challenges." For generations, one of those ongoing challenges has been "Glass breaks. Fix it." In the 1960s, Corning's scientists first invented an ion exchange technology that made glass far stronger than ever. They've since continued to invent thinner, stronger glass, even though for about forty years there was no category-defining market for it. A corporation like Corning has the money, patience, and permission from its investors to work on really hard technology problems for a long time.

But that alone doesn't create categories. In fact, corporations are weighed down by so much gravity—the deep, constant pull toward running the existing business—that they can be blind to their own technology insights. Xerox was a famous example. In the 1970s it operated one of the most legendary labs in technology history, Xerox Palo Alto Research Center (PARC). It invented almost everything that Apple later put into its first Macintosh computer, including the revolutionary graphical interface and mouse. Xerox completely missed its own technology insight and never capitalized on it. You know why? Because Xerox listened to its customers, who wanted better copiers, not something different called a personal computer. As Christensen pointed out in *Innovator's Dilemma*, listening to customers leads you to constantly build *better*, but never to build *different*. And different is what creates new categories. Better leads to a faster horse; different leads to a Model T.

This line of thinking—technology versus market insights; better versus different—circles back to the Gorilla Glass story and why Corning has been able to create so many categories. An enduring company like Corning has long-standing, trust-based relationships, and those relationships are a fantastic way to gain market insights—as long as the leadership is listening for different instead of better. Weeks had such a relationship with Jobs. As Weeks tells it, he and Jobs were talking one day about Apple's plan to build a phone, and Weeks proposed an idea that came out of Corning's work with lasers and fiber optics. Phones at the time had tiny screens, and Jobs wanted to offer mobile video, so Weeks proposed "microprojection"—a way to put lasers in a phone so it could project video on a wall. "Steve proclaimed this to be the dumbest idea he ever heard, as only he can do," Weeks told us. But that led Jobs to tell Weeks more details about what would become the iPhone. It included the radical idea of making the whole surface of the phone a touch screen. The surface had to be scratch-proof and hard to break as well as touch sensitive. Jobs thought the solution was plastic, but he couldn't get plastic to meet his demands.

Here's what Weeks heard: Jobs was going to create a new category of mobile device—the smartphone. And smartphones—all smartphones!—were going to need a new category of glass that did not yet exist.

Well aware of Corning's decades-long work on thinner, stronger glass, Weeks now had a market insight in one pocket and a technology insight in his other pocket. He told Jobs: If you create the problem (a smartphone category that needs a surface), we can create the solution (a new category of glass). Back at Corning, he told his lab and his team: if we create a solution (the new glass), we'll have a problem waiting to suck it out of us (smartphones). This is an example of the advantage smart corporations can exploit: they have relationships that give them a big window on market insights, and a set of core capabilities that can create and deploy a technology insight. In this case, Jobs said, Yes, we'll trust you to build the glass. Weeks said, Okay, we trust you to make a market for us.

From there, Corning did category design. Instead of just making a white-label glass product for iPhones, Corning intentionally created a new category of glass, giving it the brand name of Gorilla Glass, coming up with a POV about what it is and what else it can be used for, and using the iPhone's introduction as a lightning strike that would force mobilization inside the company. In 2007, the iPhone debuted, coated with Gorilla Glass. Corning set out to establish the category in all mobile phones. The flywheel dynamics kicked in, helping to make Corning the low-cost producer, smartest marketer, and the brand that stuck in customers' minds. By 2012, Gorilla Glass was on a billion devices worldwide. By 2015, Gorilla Glass was reportedly bringing in $1 billion in annual revenue, though Corning doesn't break out a specific number. The brand had category king economics, taking more than 70 percent of the category's profits.

Why did this work at Corning when it didn't at Xerox? Certainly, the CEO is key—Weeks had to buy into category creation and drive it inside the company. Employees have to be conditioned to embrace category creation and fight the gravity of their everyday jobs—they expect that this is an important part of working at Corning and how they get rewarded. Investors are conditioned to expect that some profits will be spent on R&D and category design—on building category potential instead of just harvesting existing categories. A few other points from Weeks:

"Listen to [customers] so that you understand what the root problem is rather than just doing the solution, because if we just do what we're told, they wouldn't need us, and if they didn't need us, we wouldn't be able to generate the kind of profitability and competitive advantage that it takes to define a category."

"Understand how important time is. It takes a long time to [invent] new materials. We build that knowledge, then the skills in our people, then we're able to use that knowledge to attack other markets. It's way more knowledge-efficient."

"You've got to make sure you're on the creative side of creative destruction. Because if you aren't, you'll ultimately end as a company."

We don't want to be overly enthusiastic about Corning. While Corning has proven it can create categories, as a company it is a basket of categories. Some, like TV glass, are mature and getting harvested. Gorilla Glass is a new category still building its potential, but even the category potential of Gorilla Glass doesn't seem to be enough to profoundly impact the market cap of a company as large as Corning. The stock at the end of 2015 had been stuck in a narrow range for a decade. For any big old corporation, managing a basket of categories can be a task far more complex than starting a new company aimed at a single category.

But Corning's ability to define, develop, and dominate new categories has helped the company remain relevant and vibrant decade after decade. Creating new categories renews Corning as old categories slough away. Take away category creation, and any company becomes tired and expendable—a Unisys, Alcatel-Lucent, AMD, or SAP. We believe Corning is proof that an old company can institutionalize category design. If a big old company applies category thinking, all of what we've written about in this book can happen inside the fortress. Category design is not only for pirates who storm the gates—it works for pirates already inside the gates.

The New Continuous Category
Creation Machines

In the 2000s and 2010s, Apple became the world's most valuable company because it continuously created new categories with fantastic new category potential. First came the iPod and iTunes, then the iPhone, then iPad, and maybe the Apple Watch. The question that has hung over Tim Cook's Apple is whether the company's continuous category creation machine is institutional—or whether it was locked inside Steve Jobs's head. If it's the latter, Apple could be a highly profitable company for a very long time as it eats the fantastic category potential it has opened up, but its category potential will run out of momentum, and investors will see it as a harvester instead of as a category creator.

As we write this, two legendary category king tech companies—Amazon and Google—look like they're building continuous category creation machines that will operate well after the current leadership relinquishes control. We looked at what they're up to through the lens of category design, and what we might learn from them.

Let's start with Amazon. In the last chapter, we discussed how effectively Amazon built a flywheel and continuously expanded its category of online retail, pushing out the category potential one level at a time—going past books, past CDs, and on into everything. But Amazon has also shown a remarkable hankering for starting entirely new categories outside its core retail category. Amazon Web Services (AWS) created the category of public cloud computing services and continues to be the king despite well-funded competition from Google, IBM, and Microsoft. When in 2015 Amazon first broke out and revealed AWS's numbers, it showed a whopping $6.3 billion in annual revenue, growing 50 percent a year. Analysts said Amazon's market share of the category was more than that of Google, IBM, and Microsoft combined.

Amazon's other category creation success was the Kindle e-book reader. Launched in 2007, by 2015 single-purpose e-book readers might have already run out category potential, replaced by reading on tablets and big-screen phones. But in its time, Kindle helped create the e-book market, and reigned as king of e-readers, crushing new entrants such as Barnes & Noble's Nook.

The larger lesson from Amazon is the way CEO Jeff Bezos built a culture that encourages category creation. He conditioned investors from early on to expect Amazon to fund category creation at the expense of profits. "One of the things we wrote about in our 1997 shareholder letter is that we are going to be bold with our experiments and some of them aren't going to work," Bezos said.[7] He conditioned his company to think in terms of new category creation. "There's nothing wrong with doing extensions along competencies," he told us. "But think long-term and you can see very clearly that if you're unwilling to learn new skills and competencies as a business, then eventually you will be outmoded."[8]

Bezos told a conference audience in 2014 that Amazon expands into new categories in one of two ways. The first applied to Kindle: "From a customer need to our skills." In other words, because of Amazon's relationships, it had a market insight (the need for an e-reader), but it didn't have the skills or technology to meet it in-house. Amazon knew nothing about hardware design. Undaunted, Amazon hired its way to having the right talent.[9] The other path Amazon follows into new categories is "from our skills to a new set of customers," Bezos said.[10] This was the AWS story. A Bezos lieutenant, Andy Jassy, saw that Amazon was running a huge transaction and data system, and had a vision for renting out its infrastructure and know-how to other companies. "We tried to envision a student in a dorm room who would have at his or her disposal the same infrastructure as the largest companies in the world," Jassy said. "We thought it was a great playing-field leveler for start-ups and smaller companies to have the same cost

structure as big companies."[11] At the time, such a business was almost unheard-of, and the customers were far afield from Amazon's
usual online shoppers. Jassy wrote a pitch memo and presented it
to Bezos, and got the green light to build AWS in 2003.

Bezos built a culture that understands the power of a POV.
AWS and Kindle succeeded because each started with a strong,
unwavering POV. Kindle had to offer as good a reading experience
as a book, with the advantages of an always-on connection. AWS
stuck to two key principles. One was that idea that any student or
garage start-up could harness the power of Amazon's systems, and
the second was "pay by the sip"—in other words, customers would
pay for the capabilities they use rather than contract for a fixed
amount up front. AWS's POV made it the darling of the start-up
world and won early customers such as Dropbox and Airbnb.

Finally, Kindle and AWS turned into their own flywheels inside of Amazon, building momentum, attracting ecosystems, and
driving back challengers. But those flywheels also became additive
to Amazon's larger, enduring flywheel, sometimes in unexpected
ways. AWS transformed Amazon's image. Before AWS, Amazon
was seen as a retailer that was taking advantage of technology. After AWS, it was seen as a technology company, and that has altered
the kind of talent attracted to Amazon and the permissions the
company might have to enter future technology markets. Successful new categories can change the flavor of the parent company.

Now, Amazon has also launched some big efforts that seem to
show that it doesn't always understand category design. In 2014,
Amazon tried to market its Fire phone, going head-on against
the category king, the iPhone. In September 2015, Amazon killed
the phone. One way to explain this is that the culture of Amazon has the will to create new categories and the internal mechanisms to make that happen, yet it doesn't fully use category-based
principles to sort out which ideas to chase. Building new categories could very well be something Amazon's leaders do implicitly

rather than explicitly. The company probably has a more rigorous approach to new product and business model design than category design. As result, Amazon at times falls into the trap of better instead of different.

This is one of those lessons for large enterprises: when big companies sit around discussing new products or services, one of the key tests should be whether the product or service would define a new category, or if it would be entering an existing category already dominated by a king. If big companies understood the difference, they'd more rarely spend a dime entering someone else's category.

Certainly Amazon is showing how a big, established category king can renew itself by designing, developing, and dominating new categories. We particularly love Amazon's rubric of "from customer needs to our skills" or "from our skills to new customers." It seems like a brilliant way to describe what Corning has done for generations—looking at the same time for both technology insights that come from inside the company, and for market insights that come from the views the company has on the external world. This, to us, seems to define smart, disciplined category design inside an enduring enterprise.

Google's 2015 move to reorganize as Alphabet looks a lot like an attempt to set up a continuous category creation machine—and to smartly separate category harvesting from category creation. The Google search business is one of the greatest technology kings of all time. The search business unit was in 2014 responsible for almost all of Google's $66 billion in revenue, and the company owned almost 70 percent of the search market. Google seems intent on now milking every drop out of this cash cow for as long as it can. But that takes a very different mentality than category creation, and Google's leadership clearly wants to continue to create, not just harvest. In the blog post announcing the change to Alphabet, CEO Larry Page wrote that his cofounder "Sergey [Brin] and I are seriously in the business of starting new things."[12] So Page and Brin are decoupling managing the "as-is" business from creating "to-be" businesses.

Entrepreneurial executives inside Google no doubt had become trapped by the inertial force of the search business. Gravity-bound executives work eighty hours a week doing business reviews, responding to customer demands, flying around hell's half acre on sales calls, meeting with investors, and so on. That's required to run a successful operation. The downside is that people "tinkering" on new stuff can seem irritating to executives focused on the core business. Those charged with building the next great business simply don't get much time, attention, or funding. A strategy to cultivate innovation while preserving the core business looks smart through the category design lens.

The lesson from Alphabet is that big companies need to know the difference between harvesting and creation, and set those apart. It's not easy. Investors tend to want one or the other. Google/Alphabet is building harvesting/creation separation into the very structure of the company.

Category Design vs. Kidding

Salesforce CEO Marc Benioff in 2015 directly targeted SAP, sensing its weakness in enterprise cloud software. He told analysts "we are really targeting one company to beat, and that's SAP." Then he added: "The only innovation SAP has is in rhetoric. They should try writing some software."[13] Which, we admit, made us giggle. Yet behind Benioff's attack lies a serious story about a reason big old corporations struggle to effectively create new categories. It happens when they convince themselves they're doing category design when they're actually not. We call this: kidding.

SAP was founded by five former IBM engineers in Germany in 1972. The company originally set out to develop payroll and accounting software for corporate mainframes. Over the next decade or so, SAP's products evolved into software designed to coordinate all of a company's processes, and SAP created the new category of enterprise resource planning (ERP) software. The company built the category with a powerful POV that accounting, manufacturing, and distribution applications should all work together in an integrated fashion. SAP made itself the king of ERP and grew into a tech giant, and for that we salute SAP's early leadership. By the 1990s, a large swath of Fortune 500 companies ran their operations on SAP software installed on in-house data centers.

In the 2010s, SAP found itself staring at the same looming scenario that bedeviled Siebel: If a newcomer were to create a new category of cloud-based ERP that was simpler, easier to manage, more flexible, and less costly than SAP's software, SAP would sink just like Siebel did. So some people inside SAP thought the company should try to get out ahead of this likely threat and create the category itself. Keep in mind, though, that SAP was deep into harvesting its established ERP software business, making big profits and pleasing investors with its steady-as-she-goes strategy. By its very nature, a cloud-based version of SAP's ERP software would de-position SAP's established business, which was generating all the profits from customers paying high-cost maintenance fees. It was a classic Innovator's Dilemma problem: how can you cannibalize yourself, even when you know it's the right thing to do?

To SAP's credit, it started making moves toward cloud technology. In 2011, it bought SuccessFactors, a Silicon Valley company that offered cloud-based human resources management software. Around the same time, SAP assembled a unit called HANA, which offered a database management system in the cloud.

However, if SAP didn't want to become Siebel, the whole company would've had to adopt a new POV built around cloud, and completely get behind the creation of a new category that would blow up its old category. It would've been a bet-the-company BHAG, not unlike IBM's decision to make the 360 in the 1960s. But here's what happened instead: because the company already had SuccessFactors and HANA and a few other fringe cloud plays, SAP's senior leaders believed they were already designing a new cloud category. Yet they were really just protecting the old core business while dabbling around the edges with cloud. In short, when it came to defining and developing a new category, SAP wasn't serious—it was kidding. Like the leadership of a lot of big old corporations, SAP's team stayed focused on the business of harvesting while soothing its fears by investing a little in the future but not truly committing to it. They were kidding about creating a new category that would upend their old category. The same thing happened when newspapers set up websites in the 1990s but didn't embrace the collapse of print, or when universities set up massive open online courses and believed that protected them from the forces of the Internet and cloud. SAP said it was transforming itself into a category king of cloud ERP, but it was kidding.

SAP isn't alone. Gravity pulls hard at big old corporations. Category harvesting doesn't mix easily with category creation. When most harvesters say they're creating new categories, they are kidding. That's not meant to be an insult—it's the reality of running a big business owned by investors who have expectations of certain quarterly results.

One way to get past kidding is to build category creation into the DNA of the business and condition investors to understand categories and category potential. Corning did it. Amazon and Google are doing it. But many, many companies have not done it. For the leaders of all the companies that desire to truly tackle category creation, a good way to start might be to look in the mirror and ask: are we just kidding?

How About Companies That Aren't Technology Companies?

First of all, if you think you're in a company that's not a technology company, we suggest that you read Marc Andreessen's 2011 manifesto, "Why Software Is Eating the World."[14] It will hammer you over the head with the idea that every company in every industry is now a technology company. (The alternative is that you are a soon-to-be-dead company.) Whether you make donuts or shoes, architect buildings, or operate railroads, you are now a technology company that will increase your odds of success by applying category thinking.

That said, we wanted to get a better idea of how consumer products companies—the kind that make beer or razors—think about category design. For perspective, we talked to Eddie Yoon of the Cambridge Group, whom we mentioned in the first chapter. He tracks category creation at companies like Procter & Gamble and Anheuser-Busch InBev.[15] Here's what was remarkable about Yoon's stories of true category creation inside big old consumer products corporations: he didn't have many of them to tell. He couldn't name any companies that have an institutionalized category creation process.

Still, he could cite four different ways that he's seen category creation happen inside big consumer products companies. They may be one-off adventures, but each sheds some light on how such a process can work.

Nestlé took the skunk works approach to developing its Nespresso machine. A skunk works—a small operation set aside from the main business—is Christensen's solution to Innovator's Dilemma. Yoon hasn't seen it work often. Nestlé's Nespresso started as a small project in the 1980s. An espresso-making machine didn't fit with Nestlé's food businesses, but Nestlé stuck with Nespresso, even though the unit didn't break even until the 1990s. By the 2000s, Nespresso had blossomed into a global brand.

Some big companies only create categories when some pirate inside the company decides to covertly break the rules and ask forgiveness later. Yoon said this is how Sara Lee became the first company to introduce Angus beef hot dogs, now a $100-million-a-year product. Most pirate stories, Yoon noted, don't turn out so well.

Gillette's Oral B Pulsar is more of a story about an all-hands-on-deck emergency effort. The Pulsar B is a battery-powered toothbrush with spinning bristles. In a 2001 executive review, Gillette CEO Jim Kilts realized rival Crest was trying to create a new category of tooth care with its SpinBrush. Before that, consumers either bought a cheap manual toothbrush or an expensive electric toothbrush. Crest showed up with a hybrid that landed in the middle. But Kilts was certain Gillette could do it better and steal the category while it was still unformed in consumers' minds. He ordered the entire company to get involved, and even set up an innovation fair so Gillette divisions could crossbreed ideas and technologies. The result was the Oral B Pulsar. Still, we'd argue that Gillette's effort came too late. The Pulsar and SpinBrush opened up a new category, but no brand in that space established itself as a king, which may also be a reason the category has never been a real blockbuster.

Yoon could think of just one story of actual category design thinking inside a long-standing consumer products company. In the mid-2000s, beer giant Anheuser-Busch considered going into distilled spirits to spur growth. But everything about the liquor business—manufacturing, distribution, marketing, packaging—was very different from beer. Through a Peter Drucker–like process of analyzing the opportunities in the market and Anheuser-Busch's strengths, the company came up with a new category of a popular mixed drink (a take on margaritas) made with beer (no tequila!) and packaged and sold in the equivalent of beer cans.

Thus was born Bud Light Lime Lime-A-Rita. Launched in 2012, by 2013 the brand hit $472 million in annual sales—a huge hit that established a new beer-cocktail-in-a-can category with Bud Light as the category king.

In the end, though, "[t]he words 'category creation' are not part of the vocabulary in corporate America," Yoon told us. We'd like to humbly suggest that it can be. The giants of management thinking who preceded us—the likes of Drucker, Christensen, Moore, and Collins—have long urged corporations to think boldly, fight gravity, and create the new. We believe category design is an important part of management for this ultranetworked era.

The Play Bigger Guide to Continuous Category Creation

Step One: Who?

Everybody. Of course, the CEO has to get behind category design and drive it, but the bigger the company, the more its culture has to play a role. A CEO can't directly influence thousands of employees and multiple divisions. She has to be the leader of a culture infused with category thinking, where employees feel it's not only part of their jobs, but the best part of their jobs.

Step Two: Condition Investors

Category creation can't happen when management's focus is entirely on profits and making quarterly numbers. Most big old corporations have investors who expect the company to behave like a stereotypical big old corporation, with predictable growth and nice dividends. If you're the CEO and want to become a daring category designer, you're going to need your shareholders' support—or a new set of shareholders.

Step Three: Take Advantage of Time

Start-ups have to race against time. A venture-backed technology start-up has six to ten years to become a category king, or it will likely fail to create long-term, enduring value. Established businesses can use time to their advantage. Big old corporations often have the time to solve deep, hard problems. Those solutions can turn into important new categories that start-ups can't touch. Invest in knowledge and skills over time, whether that's through R&D (Corning) or hiring new kinds of employees (Amazon), then use such knowledge to pounce on category creation opportunities when they arise.

Step Four: Listen for Different, Not Just Better

Customers will ask for *better*. You want to hear *different*. Look for what's missing, not what can be improved. No one was better at this than Steve Jobs, who practiced the art of giving people what they didn't yet know they wanted. *The Innovator's Dilemma* describes how companies get caught in the trap of *better*. But *better* is what you do when category harvesting. *Different* is what you do when category designing.

Step Five: Deploy Category Design

The discipline of category design is not just for technology start-ups. It can work the same way inside a big old corporation—or, for that matter, inside a midsize regional business, or a nonprofit, or any other organization that wants to make an impact. When you discover a category, work up its POV, develop its blueprint and ecosystem, set up a lightning strike, mobilize, and get its flywheel spinning.

Step Six: Don't Kid Yourself

Along with gravity, "kidding" is the biggest obstacle big old corporations need to fight through. Most big corporations clearly see new categories that will displace their current categories. Don't offer some underfunded, halfhearted product in the new category while protecting the profits of the old category and think you've done your duty. Better to develop the new category and become its category king than wait for someone else to do that. Your old category will get de-positioned either way.

Step Seven: Manage the Category Portfolio

Major corporations will own categories that are at different stages. Some categories will be ripe for harvesting. Some need to be created and developed. Set up a structure that allows both to thrive—perhaps a Google/Alphabet kind of mechanism— without diluting each other. Put category harvesters in charge of harvesting and category designers in charge of designing, and know the difference. Debate openly. Talk about how long you think you can harvest. Get your best people in a room and talk about how to create a new category that could put you out of business. Be declarative about your strategy—what percentage of the company is focused on harvesting versus creating. Build a culture that looks for and embraces new categories as a way to constantly renew category potential and make the company dynamic, generation after generation.

Oh, and one last thing: hire employees who understand how to apply category design thinking to their careers. We'll get into that next . . .

10

How You Can Play Bigger

Position Yourself or Be Positioned

Most of what we've said about category thinking and category design can also be applied to people in their lives and careers. It has, without a doubt, applied to us.

We'd like to tell you a story about Dave—a story that has come up time and again during our working sessions for this book.[1] Dave was an Iowa farm boy who went to an Iowa college most people couldn't name. At twenty-five, he moved to Silicon Valley with no experience, hoping to kick-start his career at an ad agency. He soon wound up working with Christopher, who was the chief marketing officer at software company Vantive. Dave quickly became valuable to Christopher, who is barely older than Dave, and they developed a tight working relationship. At some point, Dave was assigned to work on an SEC filing that had to list executive compensation. Dave discovered then that Christopher was making ten times more than he was. This was shocking to a guy who grew up believing that highly paid executives were always fifty years old and had climbed the ladder one grueling rung at a time. So Dave marched into Christopher's office. "I'm working harder than all these other people," Dave said, agitated. "You're just a year and a half older than me, you're the CMO of this company, and I don't know how I can work any harder or add any more value and I'm still the lowest person on the totem pole and I'm making shit for money and I can't pay my bills."

This is when Christopher, as only Christopher can, looked at Dave with a straight face and said, "Well, Dave, you have two choices in business and in your career. You can position yourself, or you can be positioned. And I've positioned myself as a CMO in this company, and you've been positioned as the lowest person on the totem pole."

Not long after, Christopher moved on to Scient and Dave made a decision to stop being the lowest guy on the totem pole and start from the top. He moved across the country to Boston, where he could begin anew with perceptions, and took a job as head of marketing for a tiny start-up. His goal was to do what we say companies should do: condition the market to accept him as a top-flight executive. It set Dave on a path to running marketing for Coverity.

For all of this book's authors, category design is personal. We were all once positioned as something we didn't want to be. Christopher, fighting the image that, because of dyslexia, he was stupid, could've wound up as a scraggly street musician in Montreal. Al might still be a surf bum living on Vegemite in Sydney. Dave could be tending cows in Iowa; Kevin, writing about speidie[2] cook-offs for the local Binghamton newspaper. We had to position ourselves so we didn't hand the right to do that to someone else.

When we looked at the way legendary companies approach category design, we realized that successful people do some of the same things. Category design can be a strategy for increasing your odds when the odds are stacked against you. It involves embracing the idea that you don't exist in a vacuum, and taking action to condition the market to see you in a certain way. It's identifying a problem that people need solved and offering a new way to solve it, not just doing something well and hoping that's enough. And it's about taking advantage of the exponential value of *different* versus the incremental value of *better.*

Lots of people got famous by intuitively building their careers in a way that's in keeping with category design. Muhammad Ali became the most famous athlete in the world because he sculpted a completely different category of boxer from any that had come before. He danced and cajoled in the ring and was clever and outspoken in public, plus he was always—to use his word—pretty. How many boxers before Ali ever called themselves pretty? Mahatma Gandhi could've been just another activist or revolutionary, but he invented the category of nonviolent resistance, and conditioned the market (Indians) to believe he could solve their most dire problem (getting rid of British rule) in a new way. After *American Graffiti* in 1973, George Lucas could've gone on to be just another good director in Hollywood. Instead, he made himself into a *different* director. Lucas set up shop in the San Francisco Bay area, embraced technology and computer-generated effects, and took over as the category king of science fiction epics.

But category kings don't have to be international superstars, just as category king companies don't have to be Facebook or Amazon. Category kings exist in small niches in every layer of our lives. We know who they are because they stand out, do something different, and make an impact. Their dent in the universe may be tiny, but it's a dent nonetheless.

We thought about examples of individuals who were pivotal category kings in our lives, and we're sure you can think of similar examples in yours.

For Dave, a chemistry teacher named Larry Clark made an impact by being different. In the milieu of Dave's Charlton, Iowa, high school, Clark created a category that otherwise wasn't there: life mentor. He developed a point of view: students matter, not rules or grades. His product or service? He gave a sanctuary to kids who just needed a place to get out of the high school jungle and share their feelings, and paid kids to do part-time jobs that Clark really didn't need done. (Dave says he painted the same building for Clark about ten times.) One big impact on Dave was that Clark taught him to always think of the bigger picture in times of trouble.

In Australia, Al got one of his first jobs working for John Gray, a former professor of statistics from the Caulfield Institute of Technology (since merged with Monash University) who ran a specialty math lab at BHP Steel's Westernport mill. Long before anyone had heard of such a thing, Gray had a vision for using computers for "business intelligence." He imagined a day where the people running the steel mills could ask simple questions of a database and get statistically correct answers, and hired Al to help him build a system that Gray hoped would let Western steel companies compete against the high-quality steel being made by the Japanese. His approach was wildly different, not just better, and led Al to understand that data could solve problems in new ways—which in turn led Al first to apply data to Australia's America's Cup effort and then start Quokka.

When Kevin was a teenage hockey player in Binghamton, New York, he got a part-time job with an old fellow named Harold Beam, who ran a cramped skate shop out of his basement. In his younger years, Beam had been a nationally competitive speed skater—something of a legend in town. His skate shop was sought out by every serious skater in the region. They could get skates cheaper elsewhere, but only at Beam's could they get expert counsel. Beam was the category king of elite skate knowledge, and Kevin took away the lesson that Beam did well by carving out his own *different* category instead of competing directly against established sporting goods stores.

And in Montreal, Christopher absorbed a similar lesson watching Moe Wilensky and his family, who ran a legendary deli called Wilensky's Light Lunch.[3] Christopher was eleven when his father first took him to Wilensky's. It's been open since 1932. *Travel + Leisure* magazine named it one of the Best Sandwiches From Around the World and Anthony Bourdain featured the deli on his TV show. Don't ask the servers to hold the mustard or cut the sandwich. Not gonna happen. Everyone is treated the same way at Wilensky's. The rise of McDonald's, Subway, Starbucks, and countless other massive chain restaurants couldn't impact the deli's position. Wilensky's reigns as a one-location category king, powered by one family's commitment to an uncompromising POV. They designed a restaurant niche that is different—a testament to how a small local business with a powerful POV can beat the odds, transcend time, and become a national treasure.

Category Design of Life

While reading the earlier chapters, you might've already thought about how category design can apply to everyday life. But to put a finer point on that idea, we'll briefly take you through the principles we've discussed in the book, and swizzle them so they (hopefully) make sense for you as an individual.

People aren't likely to do everything a company would do, but even just picking off a few of the principles can help you stand out, be more effective, and be more in demand. The whole idea is to play bigger than you used to.

CATEGORY IS THE STRATEGY:

The space around you is as important to your success as who you are and what you can do. You create a category to plug into when you define a new way to solve a problem that's been around, or define a new problem that people didn't know they had. If you articulate the problem well, people will assume you know how to solve it.

If Larry Clark had never existed in Dave's high school, students

and parents might not have known there was something missing—
that the school's community needed a teacher who could be a life
coach. Clark, by his actions, identified the missing element and
showed he could solve it. That made him valuable. In every school
or office or organization in the world, there are unique problems
waiting to be solved or age-old problems being solved in ways that
are no longer effective. The best way to start a category and make
yourself its king is to find one of those problems, concisely define
it, and make sure others see it as you see it. Chances are good
that others will begin to see you as the person who can solve the
problem.

For companies, we say that a category king takes most of the
economics in the category. We're pretty sure the same happens in
different ways on a personal level. If you build a reputation as the
go-to person to solve a particular problem, you will be much more
in demand than the runner-ups. At a personal economics level,
you may be asked to fill critical leadership opportunities, or be
first to be called in to fix a big problem, or be the first call from
your friends in need because they respect your opinions.

FIND YOUR CATEGORY:

We say that companies typically begin with either a market insight (they see a new problem to be solved) or a technology insight (they've invented something new and need to apply it to a
problem). Jeff Bezos has a different way of putting it at Amazon:
identify a new need that your skills will let you solve, or identify
a skill that you have and find a need.

Either way, that kind of thinking can apply to the way you find
your category. Consider your skills and knowledge, and look for an
unfulfilled need for it. If you don't have the abilities to solve it, go
get them—by taking courses or lessons or whatever is necessary.
Inherent in Bezos's formulation is a sense of harmony: the need
must match the skill and the skill must match the need. If you, as

a person, identify a problem you could never solve, that's not going to help you, just as it wouldn't help Amazon to identify a new kind of construction crane the world might really need.

And when thinking about your personal category strategy, always remember *different* versus *better.* When you seek *better*, you are moving into someone else's territory, always fighting for attention and having to prove that you're better. When two people say, "I'm the best," one of them is lying. When you seek *different*, you aren't climbing someone else's ladder—you're building your own ladder and putting yourself on the top rung. It's not an easier path. In fact, being different can be a challenging path. But ultimately it puts you in a more advantageous position than if you constantly fight for better.

DESIGN THREE LEGS OF THE BAR STOOL AT ONCE:

Okay, maybe it's a triangle, but we always default to the bar stool metaphor. For a business, we maintain that it's important to design a great company, product, and category at roughly the same time.

We think that's good advice for individuals, too. Design yourself, what you can do, and your category together. Designing yourself might involve developing a personal set of beliefs and a way of conducting your life that fits with what you do and the category you address. Design the "product"—that is, your offering to the world—by developing your skills. And design the space around you so it fits your capabilities but also challenges you.

A company's value largely depends on three factors. First is the potential market for the category it's in. Second is the position of the company in that category, because the king takes most of the economics. And the third factor is performance—proof that the king can deliver on its promises to the category. A version of that formula applies to individuals. Your value—however you want to measure it—is influenced by the potential market for what you do, your position in that market, and proof that you can deliver on your promises. All three work together. If you try to play too big and you can't deliver, you'll struggle. If you consistently deliver but don't expand your category potential, you might not grow. Consider all three factors together when making career decisions.

You can't be a category king in your career by winning the activities contest. Ten years of work is not necessarily ten years of experience. Think of your career as something to be purposefully designed. Everything you do should result in another brick you can use to build your personal brand as a problem solver, or creative artist, or as the best closer in business. Don't define yourself by activities—generate results that have a material impact on your life and use these to create and design your own category of leadership and value.

DEVELOP A POINT OF VIEW:

Here's where you put yourself on the psychologist's couch. In the process of category design, one of the most important exercises for a company is working out its POV. This work involves a deep dive into a company's psyche, exploring questions about why this company exists and what it wants to do for the world.

Putting yourself through a POV exercise can be incredibly clarifying. How do you define who you are and what you want to mean to the world? How do you want people to see you? What's the problem you can solve, and your way of solving it? Write it down and hone it until it sounds like a presentation—so that if you had ten minutes to sell yourself, you could go through your POV and anyone would grok you. Your POV defines what type of person you are, what makes you different, and why people should care. And if you live your POV, it will attract the right people into your life, and repel the wrong people from your life.

CONDITION THE MARKET:

Great category designers condition the market so it has the same aha the company had. If you are different . . . if you are identifying a problem people didn't know they had . . . then the market by definition is not ready for you. It must be conditioned to accept you. No one knew why they needed an iPhone until Apple showed them. The "if you build it they will come" mentality doesn't usually work. Apple had to help consumers understand the problems the iPhone would solve. Remember all those "There's an app for that!" commercials? That was Apple's way of conditioning the market to understand the problem, and see the iPhone as the solution.

You're not likely to air commercials about yourself, but there are plenty of ways to condition the market. At work, it might be a report to key superiors, or a presentation to colleagues, or the way you present yourself on LinkedIn or Twitter. The vehicles for getting the word out are always changing, but the point is: get the word out! And if you've developed a strong POV, you will have a message that will be clear and ring in people's heads. After all, you're trying to rearrange synapses in people's brains so they can't help but see the problem you define, and think of you as its solution.

DESIGN AN ECOSYSTEM:

A great category builds up a healthy ecosystem around its king. For a company, the ecosystem might include customers, suppliers, developers, partners, and both real and virtual communities. The ecosystem both relies on the king and magnifies whatever it does, perhaps by building add-on products or evangelizing the category to others.

People need ecosystems, too. Individual category kings are good at building a community of supporters, followers, partners, and colleagues. Do it purposefully.

Surround yourself with people you trust. Treat them better than you treat yourself. Form bonds that go beyond the walls of your company. Just like categories make category kings, other people make you successful. These are going to be the people you build teams with the rest of your career, and these people will help position you.

FIRE UP A LIGHTNING STRIKE . . . AND MOBILIZE:

When companies set out to establish a category and position themselves as king, they pick a date for a lightning strike, which is a concentrated bolt of energy meant to shock the market and get attention. The lightning strike, in turn, acts as a forcing function to mobilize the company. It creates a drop-dead deadline for everyone from marketers to engineers. They have to get everything ready for the lightning strike.

For a person, a lightning strike can be both a great motivator and a life-changing event. A lightning strike is a huge public goal, which might range from performing a musical piece at a recital to a major presentation at work. Once a date for that lightning strike is set, you will have to mobilize to pull it off. Deadlines make things happen.

ESTABLISH YOURSELF, THEN EXPAND YOUR CATEGORY:

Amazon started by selling books, nailed that, and then expanded to other areas of retail. It didn't start on day one saying it would be the next generation's most powerful retailer. Legendary category kings constantly look for ways to expand their categories, increasing their category potential. It's good advice for people, too. This is how you grow, open up new opportunities, and generate more demand for yourself. If you become the category king of product designers in a small company, maybe it's time to move to a bigger company. If you're the best kitchen remodeler in town, maybe it's time to tackle whole-house remodeling. Build on your position and move outward and upward, looking for a need that fits your skills or acquiring the skills to fit a need.

Be a category creator until you know you're "done"—when you are the satisfied king of a category that has a big enough market to make you happy. Then make the turn from category creator to category harvester. Maybe being the category king of house renovating in your town is enough to keep you going. Then it's time to focus on execution, making money, making customers happy, and making a difference. Ride that category into the sunset, and leave a good feeling behind, much like people such as Larry Clark, John Gray, Harold Beam, and Moe Wilensky have done.

Category kings start out as pirates, dreamers, and innovators. The truly legendary kings leave the scene as heroes.

So Long, and Thanks for All the Fish[4]

A book is a funny thing. It lands in readers' hands as a single, complete package, which disconnects it from time—as in all the stuff that happened over time as we worked on the book. It might seem like we knew everything that's in this book on day one, and we just had to write down the words to capture what we had in our heads. But that would not be how it happened.

We started the book full of implicit knowledge about Silicon Valley, category kings, and tactics such as lightning strikes. We embarked on the data research, interviewed a cross section of founders of category kings, and studied dozens of other companies and individuals. Once we'd done a good deal of that work, the four of us started meeting regularly for sessions at Christopher's house in Santa Cruz. We'd talk and argue for a day or two about a concept in the book, and having four of us in the house for long stretches produced some kind of magic as we built on each other's ideas and took them to an entirely new level. We liked to imagine—and flatter ourselves—that such a dynamic was the kind of thing that made the Beatles so much more than John, Paul, George, and Ringo. After each session together, Kevin would go off and write what we thought we said, and then share the document with all of us. Seeing it on paper would provoke a new round of discussion, and that would make the ideas even better (at least we thought so). Kevin would again go off for another round of writing. After a couple of these cycles, we'd wrap up a chapter and move on to the next topic.

At some point along the way, we had an existential aha. We were doing category design on ourselves.

Christopher, Al, and Dave had been advising companies for years on how to put into practice many of the pieces of category design, but hadn't really designed their own category. Our work together to describe for others how to do category design was forcing us, as they say, to eat our own dog food.[5] In order to shape the book and point it in the right direction, we had to define the category of category design (right? this gets weird, like a scene from that *Interstellar* movie). We had to understand the problem we were solving (category design can help with the need for companies to "play bigger" and increase their odds of success) and come up with a POV (which is basically chapters 1–3). The publishing of this book was our lightning strike, and it mobilized us to do the work and meet our deadlines. Ultimately, the book is the product that naturally grew out of our own category design process.

So the discipline of category design produced a book about the discipline of category design, even though if we hadn't done the book we wouldn't have so deeply understood category design in order to do the book.[6]

Why tell you this? Two main reasons.

First, we understand what we're putting you through. Category design made us think until our brains hurt. It made us work really fucking hard. It made us search for answers to questions about ourselves that we'd put off asking for a long time.

But second—it was worth it. We found out that category design is a process of discovery that leads to clarity. It did more than just produce a product. We each feel like it made us better at our work and ultimately better people. It also brought us closer together. We said in the mobilization chapter that the intensity of the process can either pull an organization apart or bond it together. The latter happened for us. All in all, we feel that category design has put us on a more enlightened path together than the ones we otherwise might have walked alone.

To finish the book, it was necessary to stop tinkering with the recipe, freeze our work, and put it in this package. But about the ideas we explore here, we feel we're only beginning to learn. We look forward to asking more questions, thinking and debating about them under the Santa Cruz sun, and hopefully helping many more pirates, dreamers, and innovators play bigger and leave some small dent in the universe.

One More Thing . . .

We want to make sure we've answered the questions posed at the very beginning of the book. In case you didn't pick them up as you read:

1. They all are or were category kings.
2. They are both continuous category creation machines. Or at least we hope Apple is.
3. Trying to win at better instead of different, and doing neither well.
4. Depends on which companies apply category design and build a flywheel.
5. Well, because he was.
6. *Category is the new strategy!*

Acknowledgments

We said in the opening line that this book is by a band, and the band couldn't have done it without the encouragement, love, support, and/or cooperation of a lot of amazing people around us.

Our band included family who were constants throughout this book. Our sensational host at Casa Cruz and chief of events, Kari Cosentino, also happens to be married to Christopher. Casa Cruz—that is, Kari and Christopher's house in Santa Cruz, California—was the book's headquarters. Kari made sure things ran smoothly and served up astounding feasts to keep us going, then also put together events that helped us spread the word in Silicon Valley about category design. And Kari's sister, Mary Forman, who is Play Bigger's ringleader, made sure everything happened when it was supposed to happen—no mean feat when it comes to us.

A next generation got into the act. Lucas Ramadan, Al's son, took on much of the data science for this book along with his buddy Will Harvey. Nearly every interview for this book was transcribed by Alison Maney, Kevin's journalist daughter. Al's niece, Leyla Van Soest, helped with our marketing and events and her husband, Max Van Soest, helped with video editing.

We can't possibly shower enough gratitude on Peggy Burke, who encouraged us at every turn, opened her home to a category design dinner event for us, and then—along with her team at 1185 Design—designed our awesome brand, website, and book jacket.

We are indebted to two legends of the book industry, Jim

Levine and Hollis Heimbouch. Jim, of Levine Greenberg Rostan Agency, has been more than a book agent to us. He's helped us shape this project from the start, and led us to Hollis, this book's editor at HarperCollins. We loved working with Hollis so much, we're now certain that no author has had a better editor in the history of books. Her touch in the editing process was smart and savvy, and we truly appreciate her constant enthusiasm for us and the project.

We are grateful for the help we got from some of the brightest minds in technology entrepreneurship, venture capital, investment banking, and academia who were willing to discuss and vet our research and thinking with us: Tina Seelig at Stanford University; Mike Maples and Ann Miura-Ko from Floodgate Capital; Bruce Dunlevie, Bill Gurley, Peter Fenton, Matt Cohler, and Kevin Harvey from Benchmark Capital; Jim Swartz, Ping Li, and Jake Flomenberg from Accel Partners; Jim Goetz, Matt Millar, and Blair Shane from Sequoia Capital; Ravi Mhatre and Arif Janmohamed of Lightspeed Venture Partners; Paul Martino, Duncan Davidson, and Richard Melmon at Bullpen Capital; Jeff Richards from GGV Capital; Joe Horowitz, Jeb Miller, Tom Mawhinney, Michael Mullany, Ben Shih, and Debby Meredith from Icon Ventures; Bryan Roberts from Venrock; Tim Guleri at Sierra Ventures; Jeff Fagnan at Accomplice; Peter Wagner and Gaurav Garv from Wing VC; Danny Rimer at Index Capital; Steve Vassalo and Mike Schuh from Foundation Capital; Michael Christiansen at Allen & Company; George Lee and Tom Ernst from Goldman Sachs; Andy Kearns, Jim Schleuter, and Pete Chung from Morgan Stanley; Robin Vassan, Jason Maynard, Ray Wang, Randy Womack, Adam Honig, Trae Vassallo, Steve Vassallo, and Mike Schuh.

And we thank all the people who granted interviews and offered their stories. You will see their names throughout the book.

This part is from Play Bigger—Al, Dave, and Christopher:

We started Play Bigger because we wanted to coach entrepreneurs and executives on how to build and dominate market categories—not because we ever thought about writing a book. Then over time a friend, client, spouse, parent, or niece would say something like, "You guys should write a book." Tina Seelig, a Stanford professor and author whom we greatly respect, encouraged us. So did Peggy Burke. So we thought about it a little.

It sounded really hard. Some people we talked to said that writing a book is the worst thing they ever worked on. We'd written blogs for Fortune.com and tech websites, but we could see that a book was going to be a problem for us. This was made clear when Dave said, "If we leave this up to us, the book will come out in 2087." The only solution: bring in a writer.

But we didn't want a ghostwriter. We wanted a true collaborator. We didn't want someone who'd just write our bullshit down. We wanted someone who'd contribute their insights.

Al suggested he reach out to Kevin to see if he would be interested. Later, to make 100 percent sure Kevin was the right guy, Dave and Christopher took on the job of pressure-testing him. So Bad Tuna took Kevin out into the San Francisco night on a quest for beers, bourbons, and bad behavior. It turns out Kevin can hang in the pocket with the best of them, even if he had to hold on to his bar stool for a little stability toward the end of the festivities that evening.

For us, Kevin has become a true partner. He's made the whole book creation process an exhilarating adventure, from leading us to the right agent, the unequaled Jim Levine, to helping find our publisher and the "classic-maker" Hollis Heimbouch of Harper-Collins, to the actual writing. Kevin is the X factor for us—the guy with the experience and unique lens required to take the musings of three lunatics and turn it into what we hope you think is a legendary book.

We at Play Bigger also want to thank:

Scott Benson, for graphics, often meeting crazy deadlines; Paul

Startz, for his work as general counsel; Joe McCarthy, interim VP of finance in the early years; Greg Finley, Larry Kammerer, and Jerry Yu, our financial team from Moss Adams; Will Ruby, for all his work on playbigger.com; Duy Thai, our trademark attorney; and Caryn Marooney of Facebook, for her strategic communications counsel.

We deeply thank the CEOs, executives, and employees who engaged with us to practice category design, which helped us fine-tune our thinking in real-world situations. Extra-special thanks to: Opher Kahane, Alon Amit, Matthew Cowen, Hugh Martin, Amy Lee, Sean Harrington, Gio Colella, Michele Law, Natalie Sunderland, John Doyle, John McCracken, Mahe Bayireddi, Adam Compain, and Diego Canales.

From Al:

Thank you to all the people who helped shape me. My parents, Tom and Lilian: you taught me right from wrong, how to raise a family, and the value of education. My wife, Christine, who had stood by me for more than thirty years, rain, hail, or sunshine. Thanks, babe. My children, Laurina and Lucas. I love you. Oh, and our dog Skittles for taking me on walks to clear my head. My sisters, Susan, Meredith, Yasemin, and Jan, and brothers, Christopher and Dave. Thank you for always being there. To the next generation: I am eternally grateful to you for taking on the messed-up world we have left you and engaging in the challenge of making this world a better and safer place. Lukie, Willie, Joshie, Charles, Sammie, Benny, Taylor, Caedran, Matt, Caroline, Skylar, Makena, Katie, Benji, and Erin: you are an inspiration and I have every confidence that you will prevail. My nieces and nephews: Leyla, Sam, Gianni, Milli, Jessica, Gemma, Jake, Caroline, Michael and Melanie, Adrian and Stuart. Thanks for keeping me current and fixing my music collection. Dear friends who have always supported me: Stuart Begg, Rob Begg, Rob Geary, Michael and Peggy Gough,

Sally and Michael Aldridge, Ben Rewis and Melanie Gideon, Matt and Stephanie Hanson, Mike and Alissa Bloch, Jurg and Brook Spoerry, Ben and Lorinda Kottke, Tim Rhode, Tushar Atre, John Taylor, along with hundreds of like-minded individuals of the Pow Patrol and the XXO crew. My business mentors: Philip Snoxall, John Gray, the late Lionel Singer, John Bertrand AM, Dick Williams, Barry Weinman, Roel Pieper, Rob Burgess, Don Lucas, and Bruce Chizen. All my coworkers who have stood beside me as we made multiple attempts at denting the universe. Special mentions to: Jackie Osborne, Carl Hartung, Michael Stavrou, and Sue Kupsch from my early days at Monash University; Bart Vijvaberg, Valery Vilsten, Heather Maughan, Brian Maughan, and Jayne Dixon from BHP Steel; Peter Morris and Grant Simmer from the 1995 America's Cup Challenge; Les Schmidt, Steve Nelson, Pascal Wattiaux, David Reimer, Alvaro Saralegui, and every single person (too numerous to mention) who worked at Quokka Sports; Betsey Nelson, Stephen Elop, Robert Urwiler, Kevin Lynch, Tom Hale, Michele Murgel, Penny Wilson, Johnathan Gay, Peter Santangeli, Venu Venugopal, and Gary Kovacs from Macromedia; Shantanu Narayen, Donna Morris, John Brennan, Tom Malloy, and Johnny Loiacono from Adobe.

From Dave:

Thanks to my mom, Miyoko, who worked night shifts for thirty years at minimum wage to put me in school and opened the door for me to have a business career. Thanks to my dad, Fred, the flying farmer, who taught me that it's okay to not follow the rules of life and still win. Thanks to Dorance and Leota for raising me the Iowa way and a bow to both my living and lost bloodline in Japan. Thanks to my brother John for pushing, shoving, and literally beating the crap out of me to make me strong inside and out. And a very special thanks to my chosen brothers, sisters, and family in Villa Hazkiel Kanaan in Beit Chabab, Lebanon, the live-free-or-die Damphousse family, the Dickenses of Singapore, the Mahers of London, Passion Jackie, Zesty, Beatty, Chambo, Jens, the legendary Colin Vincent, the one and only JJ. Osu to Sensei Shannas, Lohsen, Sergeant Ken, and the K1 family. Cheers to "I'll take Randy Moss" Blenio and the trash-talking TCFF league; to ripping all those dirt miles with Doolittle; and all those Chariton Chargers and UNI Panthers that still call me LCS. And, one final mention to my daughter Eleanor Peterson: You are the reason I go to sleep with peace of mind and wake up with a smile on my face. I love you.

From Christopher:

Thank you to everyone who loves me. Most days I feel like the luckiest guy on earth. My deep gratitude to my fierce wife, Kari—I love you, thank you for sharing your life with me BBD; you make everything legendary. To my brothers and partners, Al and Dave, my life wouldn't be my life without you. Kevin Maney, you're the X factor. A legendary partner and the missing link. This book is in recognition of my mum, Jackie; dad, Bruce; sister, Carolyn; and grandparents Catherine and John Lochhead and John (Jack) and Mary (May) Leeke. My life is the product of the laughs, adventures, dialogue, and coaching I share with legendary people. I am forever grateful to: Martin, Emma, Victoria, Madeleine Cottreau, Mary, Michael, Finn, Fox and Quinnlan Forman, Janine and David Bertelsen, Jean and Phil Cosentino, Christine, Laurina and Lucas Ramadan, Matt and Stephanie Hanson, Jason, Melissa and Joey Zappala, Tim and Tina Rhode, Chris and Kim Haas, Tushar Atre, Ben Rewis and Melanie Gideon, Leyla and Max Van Soest, Ben and Lorinda Kottke, Elliot and Elena Stone, Alissa and Mike Bloch, Jaime and Matt Lyles, Colin Vincent, Garry and Julia Hallee, Christine, Loraine and Don Campbell, Barb and David Shimberg, Alain and Deana Chalifour, Jonathan and Cherilyn Dyer, Jack Hughes, Mike Damphousse, Martin Daly, Sensei Sithan Pat, Susan Marfise and Phil Collyer,

Kristine Rose, Tom Dagenais, Skip and Jackie Jansen, Darryl Dickens, Paul Maher, Elie Kanaan, Sue Barsamian, Bob Howe, Denise and Rick White, Sarah Churchill, Doug and Denise McCullagh, Janet Matsuda, Peter Currie, Mike Homer, David Aronson, Ronn Lepage, Doug Smith, Lena and Keith Teboul, Bo Manning, George Brown, Bill Walker, Mildred, Ethel, Galdys, Betrice and Stevie Lochentino, The Ramones, Muhammad Ali, the Rolling Stones, Van Halen, the Montreal Expos, Spinal Tap, Johnny Cash, Keyser Söze, Tom Waits, Jack Daniel's, Ronda Rousey, *The Big Lebowski*, Bruce Lee, and of course, George Carlin. To our detractors and every asshole who ever fucked us over: thanks for the motivation and oh, yeah . . . BOOGER! Bless the island of Montreal, mountains of Tahoe, the waves of Santa Cruz, and every pirate, dreamer, and innovator who endeavored to play bigger.

From Kevin:

Thanks to my wife, Kristin Young, for putting up with all the trips to California and the evenings when I had to write instead of watching *I Am Cait* with her. (I am just *sooo* sorry I had to miss those shows, baby . . .) Thanks to *Newsweek* and editor Jim Impoco for giving me a place to hang my hat while doing this. I used to thank my kids, Alison and Sam, for putting up with this or that book, but they're all grown now. Alison is a writer in England. Sam is in art school blowing glass. So really, I just get to thank Pippi the cat for hanging out on my desk during long hours of writing. Finally, I can't thank Christopher, Al, and Dave enough for welcoming me into the band and into their extended, eccentric family. I've never had a better ride in my writing life . . .

None of us wanted our work to end. If we're lucky, this book will be a beginning.

Notes

Introduction: From Bad Tuna to Play Bigger

1. Play Bigger is the name of both the firm and the book, the way Coca-Cola is the name of both the company and the drink.

1: Creation Wins

1. Kevin Maney, *Trade-Off: Why Some Things Catch On, and Others Don't,* 1st pbk. ed. (New York: Broadway Books, 2009), 38–39.
2. Such is the perversity of Silicon Valley that selling a company for $20 million or $75 million is considered a whiff. Kalanick has said he was depressed after the outcome for Red Swoosh.
3. Kara Swisher, "Man and Uber Man," *Vanity Fair,* December 2014. Swisher's insightful story informs much of this section, plus we've been studying and writing about Uber since its early days.
4. Interviews with Hugh Martin, by Kevin Maney, July 2014, along with many interactions with Hugh as Play Bigger helped him with his category thinking.
5. Henry Blodget, "Here's What I Meant When I Said, 'Microsoft Is Throwing Money Down a Rat Hole,'" *Business Insider,* October 19, 2012, http://www.businessinsider.com/microsoft-throwing-money-down-a-rat-hole-2012-10.
6. The Birds Eye story gets complicated. Clarence Birdseye founded his first company in 1922, using inferior freezing technology. It failed. He improved the technology and started a new company a few years later. But not until 1930 did he launch his category-building work, selling a range of frozen food in freezer cases at eighteen retail stores around Springfield, Massachusetts.
7. Peter Thiel and Blake Masters, *Zero to One: Notes on Startups, or How to Build the Future,* Kindle ed. (New York: Crown Business, 2014), locs. 402–555.

8. "Mike Maples on Investing in 'Thunder Lizards,'" *Dish Daily*, January 31, 2013, http://thedishdaily.com/2013/01/31/mike-maples-on-investing-in-thunder-lizards/.

9. Interview with Paul Martino, by Kevin Maney, December 2014.

10. Interview with Bryan Roberts, by Kevin Maney, May 2015.

11. Eddie Yoon, "Category Creation Is the Ultimate Growth Strategy," *Harvard Business Review*, September 26, 2011, https://hbr.org/2011/09/why-category-creation-is-the-u.

12. Philip Elmer-DeWitt, "Conaccord: Apple Took Home 93% of Mobile Profits Last Quarter," Fortune.com, February 9, 2015, http://fortune.com/2015/02/09/canaccord-apple-took-home-93-of-mobile-profits-last-quarter/

13. Play Bigger Advisors, "Time to Market Cap: The New Metric That Matters," October 2014.

14. Greg Raymer interview by Kevin Maney, May 2015.

15. Adam Lashinsky, "Jawbone: The Trials of a 16-Year-Old Can't-Miss Start-up," *Fortune*, January 22, 2015. Also, as a journalist, Kevin followed the ups and downs of Jawbone for years.

16. Al Ries and Jack Trout, *Positioning: The Battle for Your Mind*, 20th anniv. ed. (New York: McGraw-Hill, 2001). This is another book—like *Crossing the Chasm* and *Ogilvy on Advertising*, as mentioned in the Introduction—that made up Christopher's business education in the absence of a formal one.

17. We once did work for SAP. As a company, it has old-man balls.

2: Category Is the New Strategy

1. Ries and Trout, *Positioning*.

2. Geoffrey Moore, *Crossing the Chasm*, 3rd ed. (New York: HarperCollins, 2014).

3. Clayton Christensen, *The Innovator's Dilemma: When New Technologies Cause Great Firms to Fail* (Watertown, MA: Harvard Business Press, 1997).

4. This is a widely held, oft-repeated anecdotal rule of thumb in Silicon Valley, but of course costs vary widely depending on what you're developing, and where you're developing it. The cost of talent in Silicon Valley or New York would be a lot greater than in Denver or Bangalore.

5. Ries and Trout, *Positioning*, 31–43.

6. "Freedom's just another word for nothing left to choose." No . . . wait . . . maybe that's "lose." Never mind.

7. Barry Schwartz, *The Paradox of Choice: Why More Is Less* (New York: HarperCollins, 2004), 4.

8. For this paragraph, we tip our hat to two sources. One is the marvelous book by Daniel Kahneman, *Thinking, Fast and Slow* (New York: Farrar,

Straus and Giroux, 2011), and the other is Cris Evatt's Brain Biases blog, http://brainshortcuts.blogspot.com/.

9. Michelle Wick, "Safety in Numbers," *Psychology Today*, July 16, 2013. https://www.psychologytoday.com/blog/anthropocene-mind/201307/safety-in-numbers.

10. Lecia Bushak, "Conformity Is Unique to Humans, Integral in Most Social Interactions, and It Begins as Early as 2 Years Old," *Medical Daily*, November 1, 2014. http://www.medicaldaily.com/conformity-unique-humans-integral-most-social-interactions-and-it-begins-early-2-years-old-308886.

11. At the time we did the study, we found 4,424 American venture-backed technology companies that had raised a Series A since 2000. Of those, sixty-nine made it to IPO.

12. We showed our findings to a number of top VCs and investment bankers, and this pretty much sums up their reaction. They were stunned.

13. Or maybe it was the IPAs?

14. Preston Gralla, "Microsoft Released Its First Tablet 10 Years Ago. So Why Did Apple Win with the iPad?" *Computerworld*, November 10, 2011. Kevin followed this in real time as a reporter—Gates once proudly showed Kevin the Tablet PC at Microsoft headquarters before it was released to the public.

15. Dan Frommer, "How to Launch a Product That Will Make $10 Billion in Its First Year," *Business Insider*, January 27, 2011, http://www.businessinsider.com/steve-jobs-ipad-keynote-2011-1?op=1#ixzz3acWzOD2Y.

16. Within a few years, it turned out there was yet another category to be birthed, in between the iPad and the iPhone. That was the large-screen phone—a category in which Apple was a follower. The new category took customers away from both tablets and smaller-size phones.

17. Clare O'Connor, "The Mystery Monk Making Billions with 5-Hour Energy," *Forbes*, February 8, 2012, http://www.forbes.com/fdc/welcome_mjx.shtml

18. If in the 1990s you had searched for "play bigger" on Alta Vista, you would've gotten any page with those two words on it. Search for those words on Google and you're likely to get us right at the top. Much better!

19. Steven Levy, *In the Plex: How Google Thinks, Works, and Shapes Our Lives*, Kindle ed. (New York: Simon & Schuster, 2011), loc. 477. We should also mention that Kevin met Larry Page at a tech conference around the time Google first launched, and Larry explained a little about Google, and Kevin came away thinking, "Why does the world need another search engine?" If he knew then what he knows now, Kevin would've invested early in Google, and now he'd be rich and not writing this book.

20. Even more powerfully, by the 2010s the category probably was no longer "organizing the world's information." The entire category could really be called: Google. Now that's category king clout.

21. Diane Greene interview by Kevin Maney, December 2014. As a columnist for *USA Today*, Kevin wrote one of the pieces that helped Greene define the category: http://usatoday30.usatoday.com/tech/columnist/kevinmaney/ 2003-12-03-maney_x.htm.

3: The Discipline of Category Design

1. A Steve Jobs construct. His oft-repeated quote: "We're here to make a dent in the universe."

2. At Play Bigger, "bag of doorknobs" has become a synonym for any company's disjointed and unexciting product line.

3. From the opening description of the book at http://www.industrialdesign history.com/.

4. Dennis Boyle interview by Kevin Maney, December 2014.

5. When Amazon launched AWS, Kevin, then the technology columnist for *USA Today*, had a face-to-face interview with Jeff Bezos. As Kevin wrote in his November 21, 2006, column, Kevin asked Bezos how Amazon was going to describe this strange new service to the public. Bezos, with a laugh, said, "I haven't figured out a way to explain this very well yet. I was hoping you would."

6. As marketing executives at Vantive, Christopher and Dave got their asses kicked by Siebel, so they got to see firsthand what it's like to fight against the category king. This led to their determination to never again be serfs in some category king's realm.

7. Marc Benioff and Carlyle Adler, *Behind the Cloud: The Untold Story of How Salesforce.com Went from Idea to Billion-Dollar Company—and Revolutionized an Industry* (San Francisco: Jossey-Bass, 2009), 23–28.

8. Gary Rivlin, "It's Not Google. It's That Other Big I.P.O.," *New York Times*, May 9, 2004.

9. One of the many reasons why we like Benioff's story so much.

10. Kevin Maney, "Salesforce.com's CEO Knows Being Quirky Gets You Noticed," *USA Today*, February 25, 2004.

11. Benioff and Adler, *Behind the Cloud*, 40.

12. Salesforce jumped the IPO sweet spot by just a little bit, going public at five and a half years old. The stock price climbed slowly until about 2009—ten years after the founding—when the stock started a long steep climb. We're tempted to look at that and say Salesforce went public too early, and that its category didn't really take hold until a decade after the company's birth.

13. Bryan Roberts interview by Kevin Maney.

14. Elon Musk, "All Our Patents Belong to You," Tesla Motors blog, June 12, 2014, http://www.teslamotors.com/blog/all-our-patent-are-belong-you

15. SAP.

4: Start: How to Discover a Category

1. Heard that Bill Gates quote? "Success is a lousy teacher. It seduces smart people into thinking they can't lose." Which just seems weird of Bill Gates to say since he's worth around $80 billion.

2. Paul Martino interview with Kevin Maney, December 2014.

3. Kind of the Silicon Valley version of the three questions at the bridge in *Monty Python and the Holy Grail*. Perhaps Dave's last question should be, "What . . . is the airspeed velocity of an unladen swallow?"

4. Kidding! There are no crocodiles in the pit.

5. Michael Fix, "Les Paul Interview," MichaelFix.com, April 2008, http://www.michaelfix.com/interviews/.

6. Ann Miura-Ko and Mike Maples both were interviewed by Kevin Maney for this book in June 2015.

7. Gene Maddaus, "Snapchat Went from Frat Boy Dream to Tech World Darling, but Will It Last?" *LA Weekly*, October 17, 2013. http://www.laweekly.com/news/snapchat-went-from-frat-boy-dream-to-tech-world-darling-but-will-it-last-4136959.

8. Ushamrita Choudhury, "The Flipkart Story," *Hindu*, April 7, 2012. http://www.thehindu.com/features/magazine/the-flipkart-story/article3290735.ece

9. Jeff Bezos interview with Kevin Maney, May 2008. It was actually an on-stage interview at New York University in front of an audience of around four hundred.

10. Miura-Ko interview.

11. Kevin Maney, "New Invention, Skype, Could Turn Telecom on Its Ear," *USA Today*, April 14, 2004, http://usatoday30.usatoday.com/money/industries/technology/maney/2004-04-13-skype_x.htm.

12. This section drawn from Ed Catmull with Amy Wallace, *Creativity Inc.: Overcoming the Unseen Forces That Stand in the Way of True Inspiration* (New York: Random House, 2014).

13. Ahead of Skype! But VocalTec proved to be too early. The technology wasn't ready for prime time and the public didn't yet embrace the category.

14. Ingrid Lunden, "Still in Stealth, Origami Logic Gets $9.3M to Help Marketers Unfold and Make Sense of Big Data," TechCrunch, November 14, 2012. http://techcrunch.com/2012/11/14/still-in-stealth-origami-logic-gets-9-3m-for-a-platform-to-help-marketers-unfold-and-make-sense-of-big-data/.

15. Opher Kahane interview by Kevin Maney, May 2015 and June 2015.
16. Actually, we don't call it the Zed. We call it among ourselves by another name, but if we did that here, it might offend a particular person. In other words, the name has been changed to protect the guilty.
17. Brian Chesky interview with Kevin Maney, 2014.
18. At the same time, Starwood Hotels & Resorts Worldwide, a top-tier traditional hotel company, was valued at $14 billion.
19. We should know. Two of our biggest mistakes involved a large German software company and a large security software company with "blue" in its name. In both cases the management teams couldn't muster the courage to pioneer new categories, even though they asked us to help them do it.

5: Strategy: The Power of a Point of View

1. Gordon H. Bower and Michal C. Clark, "Narrative Stories as Mediators for Serial Learning," Stanford University, 1969, http://stanford.edu/~g-bower/1969/Narrative_stories.pdf.
2. Paul J. Zack, "Why Your Brain Loves Good Storytelling," *Harvard Business Review*, October 28, 2014, https://hbr.org/2014/10/why-your-brain-loves-good-storytelling/.
3. At least it does not in the 2000s. In the 1980s and 1990s, under Bill Gates, Microsoft certainly had a POV. Roughly translated, it was: "A computer on every desk, all of them running Windows, and we'll bulldoze the fuck out of anyone who gets in our way." In the 2010s, under a new CEO, Microsoft is again trying to find its voice.
4. Benioff and Adler, *Behind the Cloud*, 32.
5. Ryan Marc, "The Mad Billionaire Behind GoPro: The World's Hottest Camera Company," *Forbes*, March 25, 2013, http://www.forbes.com/sites/ryanmac/2013/03/04/the-mad-billionaire-behind-gopro-the-worlds-hottest-camera-company/.
6. Not to mention their customers. How many people get excited about flying United?
7. Evan Williams interview by Kevin Maney, December 2008.
8. It's occurring to us that an awful lot of stories in this book begin at Stanford, which was in no way planned or desired.
9. Christian Chabot interview by Kevin Maney, November 2014.
10. Andrea Butter and David Pogue, *Piloting Palm: The Inside Story of Palm, Handspring, and the Birth of the Billion-Dollar Handheld Industry* (New York: John Wiley & Sons, 2002), 108.
11. This section drawn from *Piloting Palm* and from Kevin Maney's column, "10 years Ago Palm Pilot Got Started on a Bluff by Inventor," *USA Today*, March 28, 2006.
12. Butter and Pogue, *Piloting Palm*, 80.

13. We know, we know—Scient essentially collapsed by 2002. But that wasn't because of a problem with its POV or position in the marketplace. Scient fell apart because it grew too fast too quickly, and then couldn't respond and get right-sized once demand fell off after the 2000 crash.

14. We might as well throw Dave under the bus, too. In the 2000s, he launched an Internet radio site called GiveMeTalk!, with the POV of "allowing any Internet user to produce and broadcast their own talk radio show for free." The POV added: "We make free speech free at GiveMeTalk!" This was just ahead of the introduction of the iPod, and with it the concept of podcasting, which killed Internet talk radio for good, leaving Dave to suck down Jameson's while watching the rise of podcasting, social networks, and user-generated content.

15. Kevin Maney, *Trade-Off: The Ever-Present Tension Between Quality and Convenience* (New York: Broadway Books, 2010), 1.

16. In Christopher's lexicon, any high-end place anywhere in the world is known as "Chateau Ding Dong."

17. Thiel, *Zero to One*, loc. 1397.

18. Brad Stone, *The Everything Store: Jeff Bezos and the Age of Amazon* (New York: Little, Brown, 2013), 69–70.

19. Benioff and Adler, *Behind the Cloud,* 33–34.

20. When Dave was at Mercury, he was interviewing a candidate for a PR position. A big qualifier for working at Mercury was believing in our POV and mission. Quite frankly, Mercury was a tough culture that would spit you out in three weeks if you were not on board—and if you were on board, the culture would embrace you for decades. Dave thought this candidate had the right skills and was ready to meet Christopher for the "are you on board with the POV" part of the interview. But then for the first interview, she called in to reschedule due to a car accident. Dave was a tough guy, but had empathy and was fine rescheduling the interview. The second interview, she called ahead and said she was running late due to traffic. Dave spoke with her and told her to turn her car around and head home. She was stunned and asked why. Dave asked her: "If you knew there was a million dollars cash waiting for you in the Mercury lobby and all you had to do is show up on time to get it—would you have been late? Nope. You would have been camped out front of the lobby all night ready to walk in and get your prize. Working at Mercury is not a job. It's a personal, professional and career decision to join our company and be part of our mission." Dave hopes that if the candidate is reading this book, he is forgiven.

21. Catmull, *Creativity, Inc.*, locs. 1080–91.

22. Again with the Stanford thing!

23. What's the old joke? A lottery is a tax on people who can't do math?

6: Mobilization: The Shit Gets Real Chapter

1. Or God forbid the company hires some big ding-dong "Chief Product Officer" to bring in so-called management expertise. This kind of executive can be an important hire once the company becomes a category king, but not before. "Professional managers" are hugely valuable when scaling the company to tap all of the category potential. They are death to a new company or product line when brought in too early.
2. Which we mean in the most complimentary way.
3. Remember the sage words of Steve Jobs: "It's really hard to design products by focus groups. A lot of times, people don't know what they want until you show it to them." http://archive.wired.com/gadgets/mac/commentary/cultofmac/2006/03/70512?currentPage=all.
4. As we were writing this chapter, Google reorganized as Alphabet. The reason was immediately clear to us, and it had to do with gravity. Now, if Google wants to increase the odds that its new businesses will change the world, it might want to think about category design. We're waiting for Larry Page's call.
5. Rob Burgess interview with Kevin Maney, over drinks in San Francisco, fall 2014. For this section, Kevin also interviewed Bruce Chizen, who was CEO of Adobe when Adobe bought Macromedia. And then, Al was at the company in the 2000s.
6. When tech uber-analyst Mary Meeker gave her annual report on technology in 2009, she showed that NTT DoCoMo's mobile Internet growth rate for its first dozen quarters of existence was far steeper than the growth rate of desktop Internet in its first dozen quarters. Mary Meeker, "Economy + Internet Trends," October 20, 2009, presented at Web 2.0 Summit, San Francisco.
7. Alex Taylor III, "Iacocca's Minivan: How Chrysler Succeeded in Creating One of the Most Profitable Products of the Decade," *Fortune*, May 30, 1994.
8. Ibid.
9. "Chart of the Day: U.S. Minivan Market Share In 2014," The Truth About Cars, September 13, 2014, http://www.thetruthaboutcars.com/2014/09/chart-day-u-s-minivan-market-share-2014/.

7: Marketing: Conditioning the Market to Welcome Your Pirate Invasion

1. This section is built on interviews with Hugh Martin and Amy Lee, by Kevin Maney, plus our experience working with Sensity on its category design.
2. Yes—the same reporter who played a key role in Marc Benioff's effort to publicize Salesforce.com and his new category. Though we've all known

Don for a long time, we had nothing to do with his stories about Salesforce. It's a coincidence that Don appears twice in our book.

3. We want to be abundantly clear that Sensity did not try to use the marathon bombing to its advantage. News organizations, though, regularly make these kinds of connections between news events, and apparently it was the editors of the *Journal* who saw the connection between the bombing and LSN.

4. Don Clark, "Testing Smart Lights That Find Parking, Feel Quakes," *Wall Street Journal*, April 16, 2013.

5. Kevin published two previous books about IBM's history. One was a biography of IBM's builder, Thomas Watson Sr., *The Maverick and His Machine* (Hoboken, NJ: John Wiley & Sons, 2003). The other was *Making the World Work Better* (Upper Saddle River, NJ: IBM Press—Pearson, 2011), which was coauthored by Jeffrey M. O'Brien and Steve Hamm. This section is drawn from his work on those books and his research and writing about the 360 for other publications over the years.

6. Rob Lever, "Venture Funding for Startups Still Surging," Phys.org, July 23, 2015, http://phys.org/news/2015-07-venture-funding-startups-surging.html.

7. Ries and Trout, *Positioning*, 43–46.

8. For background on the Experience Curve, see *The Boston Consulting Group on Strategy*, edited by Carl W. Stern and Michael S. Deimler (Hoboken, NJ: John Wiley & Sons, 2006).

9. Richard Melmon interview by Kevin Maney, August 2015. He only had one beer when he said this.

10. Martin interview by Kevin Maney, July 2014.

11. "2004 Founders' IPO Letter" from its S-1 filing with the Security and Exchange Commission. This might be a good place to point out that lightning strikes aren't forever. By 2015, Schmidt was gone and Page was the lone CEO, the company reorganized into Alphabet so it could take chances in some divisions while protecting the core search business for investors, and quite a number of technologists, consumers, and public officials, including the European Union's antitrust officials, would take issue with the idea that Google had avoided being evil in any way.

12. We will concede that we have a little taxonomy problem here. Lightning precedes thunder, not the other way around. But we'd been using the term "lightning strike" for years before seeing the wisdom of a teaser. It seemed natural to call the teaser a "thunderclap," and only later was it pointed out to us that they come in the wrong order.

13. Benioff and Adler, *Behind the Cloud,* 43.

14. Stone, *The Everything Store*, 55.

15. Christopher and Dave were an intimate part of the Mercury story, and this section is drawn from their knowledge and observations. Both say

Some Software,'" *Business Insider*, May 20, 2015. http://www.business insider.com/salesforces-ceo-bashes-sap-vows-to-win-2015-5.

14. Marc Andreessen, "Why Software Is Eating the World," *Wall Street Journal*, August 20, 2011, http://www.wsj.com/articles/SB10001424053111903 4809045765122509156294 60.

15. Eddie Yoon interview by Kevin Maney, September 2015.

10: How You Can Play Bigger

1. So much that it's getting to be like one of those stories your grandfather tells every third day as if he'd never told it before, says Kevin.

2. Marinated meat dish found pretty much only in Binghamton.

3. Clark, Beam, and Wilensky have since passed away. As of this writing, Gray, whose father was a Royal Australian Air Force pilot, was alive and writing books about the RAAF in World War II.

4. We've honored authors such as Geoff Moore and Jim Collins. Before we left, we had to tip our hat to the great thinker and philosopher Douglas Adams, who has nothing to do with business but a lot to do with our senses of humor.

5. Or, maybe more appropriately, drink our own scotch.

6. Warning: Do not smoke marijuana and read this sentence.

Index

About the Authors

AL RAMADAN, DAVE PETERSON, and CHRISTOPHER LOCHHEAD are the founders of Play Bigger, a unique Silicon Valley consulting firm focused on selective, high-impact, boutique experiences. Together they reflect the book's title—Christopher is the pirate, Dave is the dreamer, and Al is the innovator.

KEVIN MANEY, a tech journalist with decades of experience, is the critically acclaimed author of *The Two-Second Advantage*, *Trade-Off*, and *The Maverick and His Machine*.